DOUBLE ENTRY BOOKKEEPING
AND ADJUSTMENTS

Toye Adelaja

DOUBLE ENTRY BOOKEEPING AND ADJUSTMENTS

TABLE OF CONTENTS

CHAPTER 1

1.0 Double Entry Principle

Double entry principle is the recording of a financial transaction twice in a book of account. The rule states that for every debit entry, there must be a corresponding credit entry, and for every credit entry, there must be a corresponding debit entry. It is the foundation of Financial Accounting. The recording of every financial transaction is based on the principle of double entry.

Without applying the double entry principles in accounting records, the accounting records would only reflect a partial view of an entity's record.

A financial transaction is an event which involves money or payments, such as the act of buying and selling goods and services, depositing money into bank accounts, borrowing money from a lender, and refunding money to the lender.

A financial transaction can also be defined as an agreement or a communication between a seller and a buyer to exchange goods, services or financial instruments. In financial accounting, a financial transaction (an accounting transaction) must be recorded on the books, and the transaction will be recorded differently if the company uses accrual accounting rather than cash accounting.

Accrual accounting records transactions immediately revenues are realized or expenses are incurred, while cash accounting records transactions when the business actually receives or spends money. Accrual accounting is commonly used in financial accounting, and hence it is adopted in this book.

In every financial transaction, two parties must be involved; the party that gives, and the party that receives. In some circumstances, the giver can be the seller or the lender, while the receiver can be the buyer or the borrower. Each party must keep a record of its financial transaction. The record of the financial transaction is kept in the books of accounts.

The accounting books of each party must state (contain) the accounts of a giver and the accounts of a receiver.

1.1 What is bookkeeping?

Bookkeeping is a systematic recording of financial transactions in books of accounts. It will be explained in chapter 5.

Double entry principle must be applied in bookkeeping in order to make it effective.

DIFFERENCES BETWEEN BOOKKEEPING AND ACCOUNTING

Bookkeeping and accounting are two important tools for communicating the financial operations, performances and positions of a business entity to stakeholders of the business.

It is necessary for every organization both profit making entity and non-profit making entity to record and keep books of financial transactions. Accounting is much broader than bookkeeping.

Bookkeeping involves only the record keeping aspect of accounting. It is a systematic recording of daily transactions of a business.

Accounting involves the whole process of recording, classifying, summarizing, reporting, analyzing, interpreting, and communicating of financial performances and positions of a business to stakeholders for decision making.

Bookkeeping is just a component of Accounting. Accounting is a system, while Bookkeeping is just a sectional part of an Accounting system.

1.2 What is double entry bookkeeping?

The principle of double entry book-keeping states that; every financial transaction must be treated twice in a book of accounts. The rule of double entry book-keeping states that: for every debit entry, there must be a corresponding credit entry, and for every credit entry there must be a corresponding debit entry.

When the books of accounts of a business are maintained in accordance with the rule of double entry, the bookkeeping involved is called double entry book-keeping.

The principle of double entry bookkeeping was devised by an Italian called Luca Pacioli in 1494.

Every business owner or business entity must keep a book which contains a double entry for every unique transaction. It means that in the book of a business owner, two accounts must be open for a single transaction. One account must be debited and the other account is credited with the financial transaction involved.

The procedure for double entry bookkeeping are as follows:

1. Identify whether the financial transaction involved is an asset, liability, expense or income.

2. Identify the two accounts to be recorded.

3. Identify the accounts to be debited and the accounts to be credited.

The abbreviation of debit and credit can be denoted by Dr. and Cr. respectively.

1.3 The format below could be used in recording a transaction using double entry principles.

Nature of Accounts	Debit	Credit
Assets	Increase	Decrease
Income	Decrease	Increase
Liabilities	Decrease	Increase
Expenses	Increase	Decrease
Owner's Equity	Decrease	Increase

The following are brief explanations of the format above:

1. When an asset increases, the value should be debited with the increase. When an asset decreases, the amount concerned should be credited.

2. When a liability increases, the value of the increase should be credited. When a liability decreases, the amount concerned should be debited.

3. When income increases, it should be credited with the value of increase. When income decreases, it should be debited with the value of the decrease.

4. When an expense increases, it should be debited with the value of increase. When an expense decreases, it should be credited with the value of the decrease.

ILLUSTRATION 1

Mr. Jones contributed the sum of $5,000 as capital for the new business, placing it with its bank.

You are required to record the above transaction in the book of Mr. Jones.

SOLUTION

Procedures for the double entry bookkeeping are as follows:

1. The financial transaction involves money deposited into a bank to commence business (cash deposited in the bank).

2. The two accounts to be recorded are Bank Accounts, and Capital Accounts.

3. Debit bank accounts because it increase, and credit capital accounts because it increase.

Note:

According to the question, the two accounts should be recorded in the book of Mr. Jones.

Note: The procedures above should not be written in an examination. They are meant for explanations.

In the book of Mr. Jones

Ledger Accounts

Dr.	Bank Accounts		Cr.
	$		$
Capital	5,000		

Dr.	Capital Accounts		Cr.
	$		$
		Bank	5,000

ILLUSTRATION 2

From $5,000 in the Bank Accounts, Mr. Jones paid out $850 to a supplier for the purchase of raw material required in a factory, and paid $1,350 for the acquisition of a motor vehicle. $900 was paid as annual office rent from the bank accounts.

Required: post to the ledger accounts.

SOLUTION:

Rules of double entry should be followed in solving this question.

Ledgers are as follows:

We have to reproduce initial bank accounts and capital accounts before posting the new transaction into the ledger accounts in order to make the illustration 2 clearer.

Bank Accounts			
	$		$
Bank	5,000	Purchases	850
		Motor Vehicle	1,350
		Rent Expense	900

Capital Accounts			
$		$	
	Bank	5,000	

Purchases Accounts			
	$	$	
Bank	850		

Motor Vehicle			
	$	$	
Bank	1,350		

Rent Expense			
	$	$	
Bank	900		

Notes on the above transaction are as follows:

a) Payment of $5,000 into the bank account is the contribution of capital by the proprietor. An amount used in setting up a business is called capital. Assume zero balance in the bank account, the amount in the bank is now increased by the deposit of $5,000 and according to the format 1.3 above, when an asset increases, it should be debited. Assume zero balance on capital account, capital now increases by $5,000. This should be credited according to the format.

b) All goods purchased for resale are called purchases and are recorded in purchases accounts. Purchases account should be debited with the amount of goods purchased ($850) because the purchases (expenditures) increase. Bank accounts will be credited because the bank account has reduced by $850 (the payment of raw materials).

c) Acquisition of motor vehicle will be debited to motor vehicle account because it increases motor vehicle (asset), while the payment for the acquisition by check will be credited to bank account because the payment reduces bank account (asset)

ILLUSTRATION 3

Mr. Andrew, the owner of Andrew enterprise contributes $100,000 on July 1, 2015, to commence a business, by depositing it into Bank account of the business.

Record the above to journal, and ledger.

SOLUTION:

The transaction above involves cash deposited into bank by Mr. Andrew to start a business (Andrew Enterprise)

In the Book of Andrew Enterprise

Journal Entry

Date		Dr. $	Cr. $
July 1, 2015	Bank	100,000	

July 1, 2015   Capital   100,000
Being the value of cash contributed to start a business

Bank Account

2015		$	2015		$
July 1	Capital	100,000			

Capital Account

2015		$	2015		$
			July 1	Bank	100,000

NOTE:

The owner of the business is different from the business. This is the reason why Mr. Andrew is treated as different from his business.

If Mr. Andrew withdraws cash from Andrew enterprise's bank accounts for his personal use, the bank accounts will be credited while the drawings account will be debited.

ILLUSTRATION 4
Assume that Andrew enterprise purchased goods worth $45,000 from TY Ltd., on July 7, 2015.

You are required to enter the transaction in a journal and post to ledgers.

SOLUTION
Steps:

1) In whose book are you recording the transaction?

2) Identify the transaction involved.
3) Identify the two accounts required to be posted.
4) Identify the account to be debited and the account to be credited.
5) Record your entries.

In the books of Andrew Enterprise

Journal Entry 1

		Dr. $	Cr. $
2015			
July, 7	Purchases	45,000	
July,7	TY Ltd.		45,000

Being the value of goods purchased

Purchases Account

2015		$	
July 7	TY Ltd.	45,000	

TY Ltd.

2015	$	2015	$
July 7		July 7 Purchases	45,000

ILLUSTRATION 5

Assume that Andrew enterprise paid **TY Ltd.** by check on August 15, 2015.

You are required to record the above transaction in a ledger.

In the book of Andrew Enterprise

TY Ltd.

2015		$	2015		$
August 15	Bank	45,000	July 7	Purchases	45,000

Bank Accounts

2015		$	2015		$
July 7	Capital	100,000	August 15	TY Ltd.	45,000

1.4 Cash Transactions

Cash transactions are ones that are settled immediately by cash. Cash transactions also include transaction made through checks.

In accounting, there are two ways to treat cash transactions.

Alternative 1

Where financial transactions such as sales, purchases and expenses involve immediate acceptance or payment of cash, **two transactions may be involved.** One transaction is the existence of a contract and the other transaction is the receipt of money or payment of money. According to the rule of double entry, two entries will be made for each transaction. There will be a total of four entries for the two transactions.

ILLUSTRATION 6

Assume that Andrew enterprise sold goods worth $5,000 to Mrs. Eunice on August 23, 2015, and Mrs. Eunice paid immediately by credit transfer into the bank accounts of Andrew Enterprise.

Record the above transactions in the books of Andrew Enterprise.

Journal Entry 1

Date		Dr. $	Cr. $
August 23, 2015	Mrs. Eunice	5,000	
August 23, 2015	Sales		5,000

Being the value of goods sold to Mrs. Eunice

Journal Entry 2

Date		Dr. $	Cr. $
August 23, 2015	Bank	5,000	
August 23, 2015	Mrs. Eunice		5,000

Being the value of credit transfer (Bank) by Mrs. Eunice

Mrs. Eunice Accounts

Date 2015		$	Date 2015		$
August 23	Sales	5,000	August 23	Bank	5,000

Sales Accounts

Date 2015		$	Date 2015		$
			August 23	Mrs. Eunice	5,000

Bank Account

2015		$	2015 August		$
July 1	Capital	100,000	15	TY Ltd.	45,000
August 23	Mrs. Eunice	5,000			

Note:

- The recording of $5,000 in 4 times at the same date signifies 4 entries. This is possible when there is a contract of sales, and acceptance of cash at the same time.

- The bank account above is brought down from previous illustration, and the bank transaction in the current illustration is added to it.

Alternative 2

Where financial transactions such as sales, purchases and expenses involve immediate acceptance or payment of cash, one transaction may be involved. The transaction may be an immediate receipt of cash for goods sold or services rendered.

Assume you are given the same information as in illustration 6. You are required to post necessary ledger accounts.

SOLUTION

Sales Accounts

2015		$	2015		$
			Aug. 23	Bank	5,000

Bank Account

2015		$	2015		$
July 1	Capital	100,000	August	TY Ltd.	45,000

| Aug. 23 | Sales | 5,000 |

Note: The above **alternative 2** is a short and direct method. It is mostly recommended where financial transactions are many.

1.5 Receipt of Cash/Check in a Future Period

The method applied in **alternative 1of** figure 1.4 will also be applied here. The only difference is the date of acceptance of cash.

Illustration 7

Assume that Andrew enterprise sold goods worth $5,000 to Mrs. Eunice on August 23, 2015, and Mrs. Eunice paid for the goods on October 1, 2015, by credit transfer into the bank account of Andrew Enterprise.

Record the above transaction in the book of Andrew Enterprise.

Solution

Journal Entry 1

		Dr.	Cr.
Date		$	$
August 23, 2015	Mrs. Eunice	5,000	
August 23, 2015	Sales		5,000

Being the value of goods sold to Mrs. Eunice

Journal Entry 2

		Dr.	Cr.
		$	$
October 1, 2015	Bank	5,000	
October 1, 2015	Mrs. Eunice		5,000

Being the value of credit transfer (Bank) by Mrs. Eunice

Mrs. Eunice Accounts

Date			Date		
2015		$	2015		$
August 23	Sales	5,000	October 1	Bank	5,000

Sales Accounts

Date		Date		
2015	$	2015		$
		August 23	Mrs. Eunice	5,000

Bank Accounts

2015		$	2015		$
			August		
July 1	Capital	100,000	15	TY Ltd.	45,000
October 1	Mrs. Eunice	5,000			

1.6 Advantages of Double Entry Bookkeeping

1. It provides a complete record of each transaction.

2. It provides a check on the arithmetical accuracy of the clerical work.

3. It provides an effective control of the business.

4. It facilitates the preparation of financial statements.

1.7 Ledger

A ledger is a principal book of account. It contains all the accounts of a business entity, and is kept on the double entry principles.

Ledger can be sub-divided into the following:

a) Sales Ledger: It contains debtors' accounts or accounts receivable. It can also be referred to as debtors' ledger.

b) Purchases Ledger: It contains creditors' accounts or accounts payable. It can also be referred to as creditors' ledger.

c) General Ledger contains the real and nominal accounts. It can also be referred to as impersonal ledger. It contains income accounts, expenditure accounts, and real asset accounts.

d) Private Ledger contains capital account, and drawings account of the proprietor.

e) Cash book is a ledger. It contains cash and bank accounts. It is also a book of original entry.

1.8 Balancing -off Ledger Accounts

At the end of each accounting period, the total values on the debit side of a ledger account should be equal to the total value on the credit side of the ledger. In a situation where the sum of the debit side and the credit side of the ledger are not the same, a difference between the two sides should be calculated. This difference is called a closing balance. This is the amount that is posted to the trial balance.

The process of calculating the difference between the two sides (debit and credit sides) of the account, and closing the ledger account is called a balancing-off account. A balancing -off ledger accounts can also be called closing ledger accounts. How the closing balances are presented in the ledger depends on whether the account is related to balance sheet (assets, liabilities and equity) or income statement (income, revenue and expenditure). The closing balance is called balance c/d in the ledger related to balance sheet because the figure will be carried forward to the next accounting period. Closing balance in the ledger related to income statement is called an income statement because it will be transferred to the income statement as income earned or expense incurred for the period.

If the total of the debit entries is greater than the total of the credit entries, then the account is said to have a debit balance. If otherwise, it is called a credit balance. The closing balances on ledgers are posted into trial balance. The debit balances are transferred to the debit side of the trial balance, while the credit balances are posted to the credit side of the trial balance

ILLUSTRATION

Here is an example of a ledger related to a balance sheet.

You are required to balance off the account given below:

Bank Accounts			
	$		$
Bank	5,000	Purchases	850
		Motor Vehicle	1,350
		Rent Expense	900

SOLUTION

Bank Accounts

	$		$
Bank	5,000	Purchases	850
		Motor Vehicle	1.350
		Rent Expense	900
		Balance c/d	1,900
	5,000		5,000
Balance b/d	1,900		

Note: The $1,900 is a debit balance, and it should be transferred to the debit balance of a trial balance.

ILLUSTRATION

Here is an example of a ledger related to an income statement.

Purchases Accounts

2015		$		$
Jan. 15	Bank	12,500		

You are required to balance off the ledger above:

Solution

Purchases Account

2015		$	2015	$
Jan. 15 Bank		12,500	Jan. 31 income statement	12,500

Note: The above account has a debit balance of $12,500, and it should be transferred to the debit side of a trial balance.

ILLUSTRATION 1.8a

Mr. Smith commenced a business on January 1, 2015 with a sum of $50,000 which he paid into his bank account.

He bought the following items and paid by checks immediately:

i.	Jan. 2 Motor vehicle	$10,000
ii.	Jan. 2 Furniture	$5,000
iii.	Jan.15 Goods for resale	$12,200

The following expenditures were also incurred.

i.	Jan.2 Paid transport fare	$700
ii.	Jan. 21 Purchase of stationery items for use in the office $200	

You are required to balance off the ledger.

SOLUTION

Capital Accounts

2015	$	2015	$
Jan. 31 Balance c/d	50,000	Jan.1 Bank	50,000
		Feb. 1 Balance b/d	50,000

Bank Accounts

2015	$	2015	$
Jan. 1 Capital	50,000	Jan. 2 Motor vehicle	10,000
		Jan. 2 Furniture	5,000
		Jan. 15 Purchases	12,200
		Jan. 2 transport	700
		Jan. 21 Stationery	200

		Jan. 31 Balance c/d	21,900
	50,000		50,000
Feb. 1 Balance b/d	21,900		

Motor Vehicle Account

2015	$	2015	$
Jan. 2 Bank	10,000	Jan. 31 Balance c/d	10,000
Feb. 1 Balance b/d	10,000		

Furniture Account

2015	$	2015	$
Jan. 2 Bank	5,000	Jan. 31 Balance c/d	5,000
Feb. 1 Balance b/d	5,000		

Purchases Account

2015	$	2015	$
Jan. 15 Bank	12,200	Jan. 31 income statement	12,200

Transport Account

2015	$	2015	$
Jan. 2 Bank	700	Jan. 31 income statement	700

Stationery Accounts

2015	$	2015	$
Jan. 21 Bank	200	Jan. 31 income statement	200

1.9 Trial Balance

A trial balance has both debit column and credit column. All the balances in the ledger accounts are transferred to the trial balance. A debit balance in the ledger will be recorded in the debit column of the trial balance, while a credit balance in the ledger will be recorded in the credit column of the trial balance.

A Trial balance can now be defined as a list of account balances drawn up to ascertain the arithmetical accuracy of the posting into the various ledgers. A trial balance is a proof of an arithmetical accuracy of postings to ledgers.

1.9.1 Purposes of a Trial Balance

The following are the purposes of a trial balance:

1. It provides a proof of an arithmetical accuracy of posting into the ledgers.

2. It provides a basis for the preparation of financial statements.

3. It facilitates easy location of errors.

4. It provides a means for determining whether or not the double entry principles have been applied.

ILLUSTRATION 1.9.1a

Extract a simple trial balance from the transactions below for the end of January, 2014:

$

Jan. 1	Started business with bank deposit	25,000
Jan. 2	Bought goods for resale by check	5,000
Jan. 3	Bought motor vehicle by check	2,500
Jan. 4	Sold goods to J. Morgan	1,500
Jan. 5	Bought goods from F. Jane on credit	4,000

SOLUTION

Bank Account

2014	$	2014	$
Jan. 1 Capital	25,000	Jan.2 purchases	5,000
		Jan. 3 Motor vehicle	2,500
		Jan.31 Balance c/d	17,500
	25,000		25,000
Feb.1 Balance b/d	17,500		

Capital Account

2014	$	2014	$
Jan. 31 Balance c/d	25,000	Jan. 1 Bank	25,000
		Feb. 1 Balance b/c	25,000

Purchases Accounts

2014	$	2014	$
Jan. 2 Bank	5,000		

Jan.5 F. Jane	4,000	Jan.31 Income statement	9,000
	9,000		9,000

Motor Vehicle Account

2014	$	2014	$
Jan. 3 Bank	2,500	Jan. 31 Balance c/d	2,500
Feb. 1 Balance b/d	2,500		

Sales Accounts

2014	$	2014	$
Jan. 31 Income statement	1,500	Jan. 4 J. Morgan	1,500

J. Morgan

2014	$	2014	$
Jan. 4 Sales	1,500	Jan. 31 Balance c/d	1,500
Feb. 1 Balance b/d	1,500		

F. Jane

2014	$	2014	$
Jan. 31 Balance c/d	4,000	Jan. 5 Purchases	4,000
		Feb.1 Balance b/d	4,000

Trial balance as at 31st January, 2014

	$	$
Bank	17,500	
Capital		25,000
Purchases	9,000	
Motor vehicle	2,500	
Sales		1,500
J. Morgan	1,500	
F. Jane		4,000
	30,500	30,500

A long list of information may be provided from which a candidate is required to prepare a trial balance.

The rules to apply are as follows:

1. All assets must have debit balances
2. All expenses must have debit balances
3. All liabilities must have credit balances
4. All provisions must have credit balances
5. All revenues and incomes must have credit balances
6. Capital and accumulated depreciation must have credit balances

Illustration 1.9.1b

Below is a list of balances extracted from the books of Mr. Cowbell on 31st January, 2013. Use the above rules to prepare a trial balance.

	$
Cash at Hand	5,150
Cash at Bank	6,850
Stock(Inventory)	4,500
Debtors(Accounts Receivable)	1,600
Motor Vehicles	5,000

Land and Buildings	10,000
Office Equipment	2,000
Plant & Machinery	3,000
Capital	30,000
Salaries	1,500
Insurance	1,000
Discount Received	200
Returns Outwards	150
Returns Inwards	50
Provision for bad debts(Allowance for doubtful debts)	800
Bills Payable	2,000
Bills Receivable	6,000
Creditors(Accounts Payable)	5,000
Drawings	1,750
Accumulated Depreciation	900
Rent Received	9,350

Solution

Mr. Cowbell

Trial balance as at 31st January, 2013

Date	Description	Dr.	Cr.
2013		$	$
Jan. 31	Cash at Hand	5,150	
Jan. 31	Cash at Bank	6,850	
Jan. 31	Stock(Inventory)	4,500	

Jan. 31	Debtors(Account Receivable)	1,600	
Jan. 31	Motor Vehicles	5,000	
Jan. 31	Land & Buildings	10,000	
Jan. 31	Office Equipment	2,000	
Jan. 31	Plant & Machinery	3,000	
Jan. 31	Capital		30,000
Jan. 31	Salaries	1,500	
Jan. 31	Insurance	1,000	
Jan. 31	Discount Received		200
Jan. 31	Returns Outwards		150
Jan. 31	Returns Inwards	50	
Jan. 31	Provision for bad debts		800
Jan. 31	Bills Payable		2,000
Jan. 31	Bills Receivable	6,000	
Jan. 31	Creditors(Accounts Payable)		5,000
Jan. 31	Drawings	1,750	
Jan. 31	Accumulated Depreciation		900
Jan. 31	Rent Received		9,350
		48,400	48,400

NOTE:

A financial statement is prepared from the information contained in the trial balance. If there is any additional information aside from the trial balance, both the information contained in the trial balance and additional information will be used to prepare a financial statement.

Note: If you are given a trial balance, and additional information, and you are asked to prepare a financial statement, you need to apply the rule of double entry to all items in the additional information by treating each transaction twice in the financial statements. Items of a trial balance need not be treated twice during the preparation of financial statements because they have already passed through the rule of double entry during the preparation of ledgers.

1.10 An Introduction to Financial Statements of a Sole Trader

1.10.1 An Introduction to an Income Statement

The main objective of every business entity is to realize a profit. No company intends to make a loss. Earning a continuous profit may not be very easy for an organization because of some reasons. Few of the reasons are mentioned below:

1) Exorbitant and Extravagant spending

2) Unfavorable government policy

3) Low sales

A loss may not be totally avoided in a business entity because of the aforementioned factors.

How can the performance of a business be determined? The answer to this question is found in an income statement which can also be referred to as profit and loss accounts. The income statement is a statement that shows the financial performance of a business entity at a particular period. These periods can be monthly, quarterly and annual.

Profit can be specifically divided into two, namely gross profit and Net profit

Gross Profit

How to determine a gross profit or a gross loss? When sales revenue is greater than the cost of the goods sold, we have a gross profit, but if otherwise, we have a gross loss. The sales revenue is the value at which goods are sold. The cost of goods sold is the total cost involved in putting goods in a saleable condition. Costs such as purchase cost, carriage inward, costs of renovating or repair of the product are regarded as costs of the goods when added together. Trading account is prepared to get gross profit or loss.

Look at the following illustration

Calculate the gross profit or gross loss for the following entities:

Business	Sales	Cost of Sales	Gross profit
X	$15,000	$15,050	($50)
Y	$6,500	$5,600	$900
Z	$10,300	$9,560	$740

Explanations:

The negative value signifies loss while positive values denote profit. It means that company X makes a gross loss of $50 while both companies Y and Z earn gross profits of $900 and $740 respectively.

NET PROFIT

Net Profit found in the income statement (profit and loss accounts) is the gross profit plus other incomes such as commission received, rent received, etc. less other expenses such as salary, rent paid, repair and maintenance of machinery, advertisement, etc. Where the total income is higher than the total expenses, we say there is a Net Profit but if otherwise there is a Net Loss. Profit and Loss account is prepared to determine Net Profit or Net Loss.

In conclusion, the end result of a trading account is a gross profit or a gross loss, while the end result of profit and loss account is a net profit or a net loss. Therefore, the preparation of a trading, profit and loss accounts gives us two sections called gross profit/loss and net profit/loss. The account can also be referred to as an income statement. A statement of comprehensive income has replaced a trading, profit and loss accounts, and a statement of financial position has replaced a balance sheet, according to the new Accounting Standards

ILLUSTRATION 1.10.1a

The trial balance below was extracted from the books of Gagar Ltd.

You are required to prepare Income statement or Statement of Comprehensive Income (Trading, Profit and Loss Accounts) for the year ended December 31, 2013.

	Dr. $	Cr. $
Sales		19,250
Purchases	15,100	
Lighting expenses	950	
Rent received		900
Commission earned		150
Rent paid	1,450	
General expenses	300	
Salaries and wages	1,000	
Fixtures and Fittings	2,500	

Accounts receivable	3,400	
Accounts payable		4,550
Bank	7,550	
Cash	100	
Drawings	3,500	
Capital		11,000
	35,850	35,850

SUGGESTED SOLUTION:

Gagar Ltd.

Income Statement or Statement of Comprehensive income (Trading, Profit and Loss Accounts) for the year ended December 31, 2013.

	$	$
Sales		19,250
Less Purchases		15,100
Gross profit		4,150
Add other income:		
Rent received	900	
Commission	150	
		1,050
Total Income		5,200
Less expenses:		
Lighting expenses	950	
Rent paid	1,450	
General expenses	300	
Salaries & wages	1,000	
		3,700
Net profit		1,500

Note:

We assumed that all the goods purchased were sold. Where all the goods purchased were sold, the cost of goods sold will be equal to purchases.

Where parts of the total goods purchased were not sold, there will be a closing stock normally called inventory. The closing stock should be deducted from the total goods purchased to get the cost of the goods sold for the period.

It can be demonstrated below:

Cost of goods sold = Purchases - Closing Stocks

Purchases in accounting are goods purchased for resale in a normal business of an organization.

Sales are goods sold in a normal business of an organization. Example, if the normal business of ATY enterprise is the selling of school bags, any school bag sold by ATY enterprise is regarded as a part of sales. If a computer is sold by the enterprise, selling of the computer cannot be called sales, but a disposal of an asset because the selling of the computer is not a normal business of ATY enterprise.

Note: Stock is now known as inventory.

1.10.2 An Introduction to Statement of Financial Position

A statement of financial position is a statement that shows the values of assets of the business, liabilities of the business, and funds contributed by the owners of a business entity. According to International Financial Reporting Standards, a balance sheet has been replaced by a statement of financial position.

This study needs to be demystified because of some beginners or those people who do not have previous knowledge of accounting. As a result of this, we will still make use of Balance sheet. Statement of financial position as required by International Financial Reporting Standards will be dealt with in our subsequent studies.

ILLUSTRATION 1

Refer to **Trial Balance of Gagar Ltd. in "illustration 1.10.1a".**
You are required to prepare a balance sheet as at that date.

Suggested Solution:

Gagar Ltd.

Statement of Financial Position (Balance Sheet as at December 31, 2013)

	$	$
Assets		
Fixed Assets:		
Fixtures & Fittings		2,500
Current Assets:		
Cash	100	
Bank	7,550	
Accounts Receivable	3,400	
	11,050	
Less:		
Current Liabilities		
Accounts Payable	4,550	
Working Capital		6,500
		9,000
Capital	11,000	
Net Profit	1,500	
	12,500	
Less Drawings	(3,500)	
		9,000

CHAPTER 2

Assets, Equity and Liabilities

Assets

In an accounting for beginners, an asset can be defined in the
following ways:
- An Asset can be defined as an economic resource acquired and
  owned by an individual or a business entity.
- It can be defined as property, and valuable items belonging to a
  business entity, such as cash, inventory, machinery that can be used
  to produce goods or other things, office building from which primary
  operation of the business is being carried out, and business image
  that makes people to patronize your business.
- Asset can also be defined as item possessed by a business entity
  from which future economic benefits are expected to flow to the
  company.

> According to International Accounting Standard Board; an asset
> is a resource controlled by an entity as a result of past events and
> from which future economic benefits are expected to flow to the
> entity (IASB).

Assets can be classified into Current Assets and Non- Current Assets
(Fixed Assets). The distinction between current assets and non -
current assets can be based on the length of time in which the future
economic benefits from the assets are expected to flow to the
business entity. The difference between the current assets and non -
current assets can be determined by the period of time in which
assets will be used for business activity.

Current Assets are assets that a company is expected to use within
one year from the date of reporting.

Non-currents assets are assets from which economic resources are
expected to flow to the business for more than a year.

All assets are recorded in the balance sheet. Non-current assets are different from current assets because they are depreciated either monthly or annually. The values of depreciation are treated as depreciation expenses in the **profit and loss accounts** for each year.

Types and Classification of Assets

Assets	Classification	Description
Plant and Machinery	Non-current	Used for the production of goods and services
Motor Vehicle	Non-current	Used for the carriage of goods and commuting staff
Computer Equipment	Non-current	Used for the processing of data and keeping of files
Office Building	Non-current	It is a place in which daily business activities are being carried out
Inventory	Current	Materials or stocks awaiting sales
Cash	Current	Cash at hand or in the office
Receivables	Current	Money owed by customers

Non-Current Assets can also be subdivided into two. The two types of non-current assets are:
i.   Tangible Fixed Assets
ii.   Intangible Fixed Assets

Tangible Fixed Assets are assets that exist in physical form such as land and buildings, equipment, plant and machinery and long term financial investment. Tangible assets are assets that can be seen and touched.

Intangible Assets are assets that do not exist in physical form. Assets such as Goodwill, patent right, copyrights and trademarks are intangible assets.

EQUITY

Equity is the amount of funds or assets invested by owners of business in the business. It is the net worth of the business. It is the capital that remains after all liabilities have been paid from the assets. It can be demonstrated by an accounting equation.

Assets – Liabilities = Equity

From the equation above, we can say that equity is the net worth of a business entity. According to (IASB), Equity is the residual interest in the assets of a company after deducting all liabilities.

Equity comprises the following:
1. Common stocks or Ordinary Shares
2. Preferred Stocks or Preference Shares (irredeemable)
3. Retained Earnings
4. Revaluation Surplus

Equity may increase or decrease at each particular period based on what happens to any of the components of equity. For example, if any of the components of equity listed above increases, there will be an impact of the increase on equity, and if any of the components of equity decreases, there will be an impact of the decrease on equity.

All equities are posted to balance sheet.

LIABILITIES

From a lay person viewpoint, a liability is an obligation you owed another person. It is an obligation of an individual or a business entity to pay cash or other resources to another party. It is a promise made by an entity to pay back other parties for the use of their assets. One of the most acceptable definitions of a liability is the one used by International Accounting Standards Board (IASB). According to the IASB, a liability is a present obligation of an enterprise arising from past events, the settlement of which is expected to result in an outflow from the enterprise of resources embodying economic benefits.

Liabilities can be classified as current liabilities, and Long-term liabilities (Non- current liabilities) based on their timing differences. The due date of payment for current liability is within a year, while that of Long-term liability is more than a year. All liabilities are posted to balance sheet. The followings are the brief explanations of each item of liabilities

Bank Overdraft: It is an extra amount of money you withdrew from your bank account aside from the original bank balance. It is a current liability.

Short -term Bank Loan: It is the money borrowed by an entity from a bank. It is a current liability.

Accounts Payable: They are the total values of goods sold to you on credit by suppliers. They are current liabilities.

Long –term Bank Loan: It is an amount of money you borrowed from a financial Institution. It is a long-term liability.

Debenture: It is a certificate of agreement of loan issued by the lender to the borrower. It is a long-term liability.

Accrued Wages & Salaries: They are the wages and salaries owed to workers. They are current liabilities.

Accrued Tax: It is the tax owed for the year. It is a current liability.

Unclaimed Dividends: They are the dividends owed to the owners of a company. They are current liabilities.

CHAPTER 3

Accounting Equation

Accounting equation is an appropriate equation that demonstrates the principle of double entry bookkeeping.

Accounting equation can be demonstrated below:

1. Assets = Capital + Liabilities

2. Assets = Owners' equity + Liabilities

3. Assets = Shareholders' Equity + Liabilities

Accounting equation can be represented in any of the above equations. The kind of ownership of a business determines the suitable equation to be used for the business. The equation "1" is a general accounting equation. Equation "2" is meant for a sole proprietorship business while equation "3" is meant for a limited liability company.

What the business owns minus what the business owed will be equal to the capital. The equation which shows what the business owns, what the business owed, and the net worth of the business or owners' equity is called an **accounting equation**.

The following two statements are important if you are setting up a business:

1) You have to contribute personal financial resources for the starting up of the business.

2) You can also obtain funds from external sources.

Where statement "1" alone is applicable, and statement "2" is excluded in setting up a business; we say a business is financed by capital contributed by the owner. This can be demonstrated by:
Resources in the business = Resources supplied by the owner

The financial resources contributed by the owner of the business are called capital, while the summation of all financial resources in the business is referred to as Assets.
The accounting equation where a business is financed by capital contributed by the owner is:

Assets = Capital

It means that the whole business is solely financed by the owner of the business.
Where statement "1" and statement two above are applicable together, the accounting equation will change to:

Assets = Capital + Liabilities

Liabilities are the funds provided by the people other than the owner of the business. The owner of the business is indebted to the providers of the finance, and hence he has to pay them back.

From the above, we can conclude that total assets can be divided into the financial resources supplied by the owner of the business and funds contributed by people other than the owner of the business. The two sides of every accounting equation will always be equal to each other no matter how you present it. The equation is the foundation for double entry bookkeeping in accounting.

Example

Mr. Jackson contributed $2,000 on the 2nd of February, 2012 as capital for a new business, placing it with a bank on the same date. He obtained a loan of $800 from a friend on the 3rd of February, 2012. He acquired computer equipment by paying check of $2,600 and he is having a cash balance of $200 in his bank account (bank balance) at the end of the Month. You are required to represent the above information in an accounting equation.

Solution:

Assets = Owner's Equity + Liabilities
Computer equipment + Bank balance = Owner's Equity + Liabilities
$$\$2,600 + \$200 = \$2,000 + \$800$$
$$\$2,800 = \$2,800$$

From the above, total assets are $2,800. The total assets comprise of computer equipment and bank balance. The capital contributed to start the business is owner's equity while the loan he obtained from a friend is recognized as a liability.

If any of the components of the accounting equation above changes, there will be an impact of the change on other components. For example, if owner's equity increases by $100, Assets also will be increased by $100. This is one of the applications of double entry principle. The principle states that for every debit entry, there must be a corresponding credit entry, and for every credit entry there must be a corresponding debit entry.

A statement of financial position is not the first statement to be prepared in accounting, but for the simplicity of our study, we will start with it. We will only bypass the accepted procedures of the recording of financial transactions for easy understanding of accounting equation. Each of these procedures will be discussed in details in our subsequent studies. The procedures we are going to by-pass are as follows:

1. Journal Entries
2. Ledgers Entries
3. Preparation of trial balance

4.   Income statement

Lets us now start our illustration with the statement of financial position.

1. Introduction of Capital

On July 1, 2013, Mr. Smith started a business by depositing $80,000 into a bank account specially opened for the business. You are required to prepare a statement of financial position for this transaction.

The effect of this transaction is an increase of bank deposit of $80,000 and an increase of capital contributed by Mr. Smith.

The statement of financial position will be as follows:

Mr. Smith

Statement of financial position as at 1st July, 2013.

	$
Asset:	
*Cash at bank	80,000
***Capital**	80,000

This is always the way information is presented in the statement of financial position.

2. Acquisition of an asset

On 15th July, 2013, Mr. Smith acquired office premises for $41,000, and paid by check immediately.
Record this transaction in a statement of financial position.

Solution

The effect of this transaction is that cash in the bank will be reduced by $41,000 and non-current asset (office premises) increases by $41,000.

Mr. Smith
Statement of financial Position as at 15th July 2013

	$
Asset:	
*Office premises	41,000
*Cash at bank (80,000 - 41,000)	<u>39,000</u>
	<u>**80,000**</u>
Capital	<u>**80,000**</u>

3. Purchase of an asset on credit

On 17th July, 2013, Mr. Smith bought goods from D. Dandy for $20,000 and promised to pay him next month. Record this in a statement of financial position.
The effect of this is that assets will increase and liability also will increase.

Mr. Smith
Statement of financial position as at 17th July, 2013

$

Asset:

Office premises	41,000
*Inventory	20,000
Cash at bank	39,000
	100,000

Liabilities

*Accounts payable	(20,000)
Net Asset	80,000

Capital	80,000

4. Sales of current asset for immediate payment

On 19th July, 2013, Mr. Smith sold goods which cost $1,500, for cost price to ZP Ltd who paid immediately by check.
Record this transaction in the statement of financial position.

The effect which this transaction will have on the equation is that one asset (cash at bank) will increase while another asset (inventory) will decrease.

Statement of financial position as at 19th July,2013.

	$
Assets:	
Office premises	41,000
*Inventory (20,000- 1,500)	18,500
*Cash at bank (39,000 +1,500)	40,500
	100,000

Liabilities

  Accounts payable   (20,000)

                                       <u>80,000</u>

    Capital   <u>80,000</u>

5. Sales of a current asset on credit

On the 25th July, 2013, Mr. Smith sold goods which cost $500 to Mrs. Jeff at the same cost price of $500.
How will the transaction appear on the statement of financial position?

The effect of this transaction will be an increase in asset (Accounts receivable) and a decrease in an asset (Inventory)

<u>Statement of financial position as at 25th July,2013</u>

                                     $

Asset:

  Office Premises   41,000

  *Inventory (18,500 – 500)   18,000

  *Accounts receivable   500

  Cash at Bank   <u>40,500</u>
                                  100,000

Liabilities:
  Accounts payable   <u>(20,000)</u>
                                  <u>80,000</u>

Capital	80,000

6. Collection of a liability

On the 26th July 2013, Mr. Smith received a check worth $400 from Mrs. Jeff for part payment of her debt.

The recording of this transaction is to increase (asset) cash at bank and decrease asset (accounts receivable).

Statement of financial position as at 26th July 2013

	$
Assets:	
Office Premises	41,000
Inventory	18,000
*Accounts receivable (500 – 400)	100
*Cash at bank (40,500 + 400)	40,900
	100,000
Liabilities:	
Accounts payable	(20,000)
	80,000
Capital	80,000

7. Payment of a liability

On the 28th July 2013, Mr. Smith paid a check of $15,000 to D. Dandy for goods purchased from him on credit.

The effect that this transaction will have on the accounting equation is that, Asset (cash at bank) will decrease, and the liability (accounts payable) will decrease.

Statement of Financial Position as at July 30, 2013

	$
Assets:	
Office Premises	41,000
Inventory	18,000
Accounts receivable	100
*Cash at bank (40,900 –15,000)	25,900
	85,000
Liabilities:	
*Accounts payable (20,000 - 15,000)	(5,000)
	80,000
Capital	80,000

CHAPTER 4

THE EFFECT OF PROFIT OR LOSS ON CAPITAL

Profit in an accounting perspective is the amount by which revenue is higher than the sum of all costs incurred to generate the profit. Revenue is the sales value of goods sold. It can also be called an income earned from a service rendered. Revenue from goods sold is the unit price of each commodity multiplied by the number of units sold. There are two major types of profit. They are gross profit and net profit.

Gross profit is the revenue minus the direct cost of goods sold. Net profit is the revenue minus the total direct cost of goods sold, and indirect expenses (overhead) incurred during the time of earning the revenue. To be precise, we can say that net profit is a gross profit minus indirect expenses.

How Does Profit or Loss Affect Capital?

The profit we are talking about here is the net profit. The capital at every beginning of an accounting period is called opening capital. At the end of an accounting period, the capital becomes closing capital.

If a net profit is made during an accounting year, the profit will be added to the opening capital to get the closing capital for the year. The effect of the profit earned during the year is to increase the capital at the end of the year (closing capital). If a net loss is made during the accounting period, the loss will be deducted from the opening capital to get the closing capital. The effect of the loss is to decrease the capital.

The effect can be demonstrated below:

Opening capital + Net Profit = Closing Capital

Opening Capital – Net Loss = Closing Capital

Illustration1

Ajax Ltd., a dealer of home appliances realized revenue of $100,000
on the 5th of January, 2014 from the sales of home appliances during
the month. The cost of the goods sold is $69,000. Indirect expenses
of $21,000 were incurred to generate the sales in the same month.
The company has a capital of $250,000 as at 1st January, 2014.
You are required to calculate the capital as at 31st January 2014.

Suggested Solution:

Calculation of Net profit:

	$
Sales	100,000
Less: cost of goods sold	69,000
Gross Profit	31,000
Less: Indirect expenses	21,000
Net Profit	10,000

The Net profit is $10,000.

We can now calculate the capital as at 31st January, 2014 (closing
capital).

Opening capital + Net Profit = Closing capital

$250,000 + $10,000   = $260,000

The capital as at 31st January, 2014 is $260,000. We can see that
when profit is realized in a period, the capital will be increased by
the amount of the profit.

ILLUSTARTION 2

Lets us use the same question in illustration 1, but assume the expenses increased to $36,000. You are required to calculate the capital at the end of the month (as at 31st January, 2014).

Solution:

Step1: Calculate the Net profit or Loss.

	$
Sales	100,000
Less: Cost of Goods Sold	69,000
Gross Profit	31,000
Less: Expenses	36,000
Net loss	(5,000)

Step 2: Determine the capital as at the end of the month.

Opening capital – Net Loss = Closing Capital
$250,000 - $5,000   = $245,000

The capital at the end of the month is $245,000. We can see that the capital decreases from $250,000 to $245,000 because net loss is a negative figure and always reduces the capital.

In conclusion, we can say that Net profit increases capital and Net loss decreases the capital. **As we have earlier discussed**, capital can also be referred to as owners' equity or shareholders' equity.

CHAPTER 5

5. Books of Accounts and Bookkeeping

Bookkeeping is a systematic recording of financial transactions in the books of accounts of a business. It starts from the issuing of source documents and ends with the preparation of a trial balance.

The various stages involved in bookkeeping are:
- Issuing of Source documents
- Recording the source documents to their respective books of original entry.
- Recording the books of original entry to their respective ledgers
- Posting the ledger balances into a trial Balance

5.1 Source Documents

It is important to explain the meaning of a business activity before we proceed with the definition of source documents. A business activity is a financial transaction that occurs during a daily business of an enterprise or a company. It can also be referred to as a financial transaction or a business transaction.

During a daily business activity, an evidence showing authenticity of a financial transaction is generated. The paper proof generated each time a business transaction takes place is called a source document or a business document. In a business transaction, a source document is an evidence that shows that a financial transaction has actually occurred. For example, if a business issues a check to a supplier of computer systems in payment for the supply, and the supplier at the same time issues a receipt acknowledging the collection of the check, the check, and the receipt are source documents.

Source documents are the documents issued each time there is an accounting or a business transaction. It is the only evidence that can be used to prove that a business transaction has actually taken place. Every financial or accounting transaction starts with source documents. The following are the examples of accounting source documents:

5.1.1 SALES INVOICE OR SUPPLIER'S INVOICE

It is a document sent by the seller to the buyer showing an evidence of goods supplied on credit. It shows evidence of **credit sales.** It is used to inform the consumer of the type, number, price, and value of the goods supplied to him or her on credit. It provides a very good evidence of a contract of sales, and it can be produced in the court of law for litigation.

 The duplicate of the invoice is retained by the supplier for accounting records. It is used by the supplier to record sales day book. The original copy always goes to the purchaser as earlier mentioned and thus becomes his accounting record and forms the basis of recording his purchases day book.

Specimen of a Sales Invoice

Exhibit 5.1.1

Samotex Ltd

No. 5, Obasa, Oyo Rd., Ib. Nig.

Sales Invoice

Your Sales Order: 12/B/120
Invoice No. 221
Date: 7/12/14
To:
Adekunle
No. 10, Adeyemo,
Oluyole, Ib. Nig

	Unit Price $	Qty	Total $
Bags of Wheat	2,000	3	6,000
Bags of Rice	9,000	4	36,000
Bags of Semo	2,500	3	7,500
Total			49,500

Amounts in words: Forty nine thousand and five hundred dollars only.

Customer's Signature	Supplier's Signature
Adekunle	Samotex

5.1.2 DELIVERY NOTE

It is a document acknowledging the delivery of goods, and that the goods are in good condition to the buyer. It is frequently called goods delivery note. Delivery note does not contain prices. It contains quantities of goods only.

Specimen of a Delivery Note

Exhibit 5.1.2

Samotex Ltd
No. 5, Obasa, Oyo Rd., Ib. Nig.

Delivery Note

Delivery Note No. 221
Date: 7/12/14

To:
Adekunle
No. 10, Adeyemo,
Oluyole,Ib. Nig

	Qty
Bags of Wheat	3
Bags of Rice	4
Bags of Semo	3
Total	10

Customer's Signature   Supplier's Signature
Adekunle   Samotex

5.1.3 CREDIT NOTES OR CREDIT MEMO

A credit note is always made out by the supplier of goods when customers returned goods which are unsatisfactory. It can also be used to give an allowance where goods are not actually returned, but are for some reasons not worth the full invoice price as a result of the goods being slightly damaged in transit.

It is called a credit note because the account of the customer will be credited with the amount of allowance to show a reduction in the amount owed.

Credit notes are often printed in red to stop them from being mistaken for invoice.

Assume that Mr. Adekunle returned a bag of wheat to Samotex Ltd, the seller on the 28th December, 2014.

Specimen of a Credit Note

Exhibit 5.1.3

```
Samotex Ltd
No. 5, Obasa, Oyo Rd., Ib. Nig.

                        Credit Note No.: 7/22
Date: 28/12/14



    To:
    Adekunle
    No. 10, Adeyemo,
    Oluyole,Ib. Nig

                            Unit
                            Price $    Qty   Total $
    Bag of Wheat            2,000       1    2,000

  Amount in words: Two thousand dollars

  Customer's Signature      Supplier's Signature
        Adekunle                  Samotex
```

5.1.4 DEBIT NOTES

Goods bought from a seller previously may be returned to the seller if the seller agrees. When this occurs, the customer will issue a document called a debit Note to the seller detailing the description of the goods and the reason for the return. It can also be issued by the seller, especially, when an invoice is made out incorrectly and the value of the transaction is being understated. When this occurs, it is normal to correct the error by sending a debit note to the customer.

Exhibit 5.1.4

```
Samotex Ltd
No. 5, Obasa, Oyo Rd., Ib. Nig.

Debit Note No.: 8/33
Date: 28/12/14


To:
P. Smith
No. 10, Aluko,
Oluyole,Ib. Nig

                                Unit
                                Price $    Qty    Total $
            Packet of indomie    2,000      1     2,000

Amount in words: Two thousand dollars

Customer's Signature        Supplier's Signature
    P. Smith                     Samotex
```

SALES RECEIPT

It is used to acknowledge the receipt of money from customers. It is given to customers when customers actually pay for the goods purchased.

VOUCHER

It is an evidential material for the payment of money by a business.

DEPOSIT SLIP

This is a document that serves as an evidence of cash deposited into bank accounts.

WITHDRAWAL SLIP

It is a document used to withdraw cash from a savings account by the owner of the bank accounts.

CHECK

It is used to pay for goods and services. It is used to withdraw money from a current account by the bearer of the check.

COMPUTER GENERATED RECEIPT

It is a document generated from computer showing an evidence of money received from customers.

In conclusion, evidence is produced each time a business transaction takes place. The paper evidence is called a source document or a business document or an accounting source document. A proof of every business or financial transaction is called a source document. The examples mentioned above are not exhaustive. There are still many more examples of source documents.

5.2. Original Books of Accounts

In order to comply with a systematic recording of a financial transaction, the information extracted from each source document would be transferred to respective books of original entry.

When a business is initially started with few transactions, one or two books of accounts can still be kept for the recording of the business. Where a business is becoming larger, many books of accounts need to be kept for easy and proper accounting.

Books of Original Entry are the books in which all accounting transactions are first recorded. These books show daily description of each business transaction. A respective transaction is entered on each appropriate book. For example, cash is recorded on a cash book. Details of transactions such as names and addresses of buyers are revealed by the books of original entry.

Posting to ledgers are made from each book of original entry.

5.2.1 Types of books of original entry

Books of original entries are referred to as journals or day books. Some frequently used books of original entry are as follows:

1) Sales journal or Sales day book
2) Purchases journal or Purchases day book
3) Returns inwards journal or Returns inwards day book
4) Returns outwards journal or Returns outwards day book
5) Cash book
6) General journal

1. Sales journal is used to record goods sold on credit.
2. Purchases journal is used to record goods purchased on credit.
3. Returns inwards journal is used by a supplier to record goods returned by customers.
4. Returns outwards journal is used to record goods returned to the supplier.
5. Cash book is used to record receipts and payments of cash and check.
6. General journal contains accounting information that cannot be found in other books of original entry. It can also be called journal. General journal is used for the following:
   - The purchase and sale on credit of fixed assets
   - Writing-off bad debts
   - Correction of accounting errors
   - Opening entries. These are the entries needed to open a new set of accounts

- Adjustment for any of the entries in the ledger.

It is necessary to distinguish between trade discounts and cash discounts before we make illustrations of recording to journals or day books.

5.2.2 Trade Discount and Cash Discount

A trade discount is a reduction in a price of a commodity. It is aimed at encouraging patronage. It is commonly allowed on slow moving and expensive goods. A trade discount is a reduction on the catalogue price of an item to enable a retailer to make profit.

Since a trade discount is simply a way of calculating sales, **no entry for trade discount should be made in the double entry records, nor in the sales day book. It is not recorded in the ledger accounts.**

Cash Discount

A cash discount is a reduction in the price of a commodity as a result of prompt payment. It is aimed at encouraging quick payments. It is given by the seller to the buyer. Unlike trade discount, it is posted to a ledger.

5.3 Sales Invoices, Sales Day Book and Ledgers

The information in the sales invoice is posted to sales day book or sales journal. **Sales Invoice** contains only credit sales. All the sales in the sales invoices will be posted to **Sales Day Book** and information in the sales day book will be posted to **sales ledger** and **general ledger**.

Example 5.3

An example of posting credit sales

Note: Assume that the following source documents (sales invoices) are issued by Samotex Ltd. (the seller) to its customers:

Exhibit 5.3a

Samotex Ltd
No. 5, Obasa, Oyo Rd., Ib. Nig.

Sales Invoice

Your Sales Order:12/B/120
Invoice No. 221

14 December, 2014

To:
Adekunle
No. 10, Adeyemo,
Oluyole,Ib. Nig

	Unit Price $	Qty	Total $
Bags of Wheat	2,000	3	6,000
Bags of Rice	9,000	4	36,000
Bags of Semo	2,500	3	7,500
Total			49,500

Amounts in words: Forty nine thousand and five hundred dollars only

Customer's Signature	Supplier's Signature
Adekunle	Samotex

Exhibit 5.3b

Samotex Ltd
No. 5, Obasa, Oyo Rd., Ib. Nig.

Sales Invoice

Your Sales Order:12/B/121
Invoice No. 222

14 December, 2014

To:
P. Smith
No. 10, Aluko,
Oluyole,Ib. Nig

	Unit Price $	Qty	Total $
Sachets of Spagetti	100	20	2,000
Packets of indomies	2,000	2	4,000
Bags of Semo	2,500	2	5,000
Total			11,000

Amounts in words: Eleven thousand dollars only

Customer's Signature	Supplier's Signature
P.Smith	Samotex

Exhibit 5.3c

Samotex Ltd
No. 5, Obasa, Oyo Rd., Ib. Nig.

Sales Invoice

Your Sales Order:12/B/122
Invoice No. 223
15 December, 2014

To:
Opeyemi
No. 10, Adeyemo,
Oluyole,Ib. Nig

	Unit Price $	Qty	Total $
Bags of Wheat	2,000	3	6,000

Amounts in words: Six thousand dollars only.

Customer's Signature	Supplier's Signature
Opeyemi	Samotex

Exhibit 5.3d

Samotex Ltd
No. 5, Obasa, Oyo Rd., Ib. Nig.

Sales Invoice

Your Sales Order:12/B/122
Invoice No. 224
28 December,2014

To:
R. Robbert
No. 15, Adeyemo,
Oluyole,Ib. Nig

	Unit Price($)	Qty	Total($)
Bags of Wheat	2000	30	60,C00
Less 15% trade discount			-9,C00
			51,C00

Amounts in words: Fifty one thousand dollars only.

Customer's Signature	Supplier's Signature
R. Robert	Samotex

SOLUTION:

The accounting information in the sales invoice will be first posted to sales day book.

Note:

Trade discount is a reduction on the catalogue price of an item to enable the retailer to make profit.

Since trade discount is simply a way of calculating sales, **no entry for trade discount should be made in the double entry records, or in the sales day book. It is not recorded in the ledger accounts.**

Sales day book of Samotex Ltd

Sales Day Book   (page 30)

Date	Names	Invoice No.	Folio	Amount
2014				$
Dec. 14	A. Adekunle	221	SL08	49,500
Dec. 14	P. Smith	222	SL10	11,000
Dec. 15	O. Opeyemi	223	SL14	6,000
Dec. 28	R. Robbert	224	SL16	51,000
Transfer to Sales Account			GL124	117,500

Sales Ledger

A. Adekunle   (page08)

2014		Folio	$	
Dec.14	Sales	SB30	49,500	

P. Smith   (page 10)

2014		Folio	$	

Dec.14　Sales　SB30　11,000

O. Opeyemi　　　　　　　(page 14)

2014		Folio	$
Dec.15	Sales	SB30	6,000

R. Robbert　　　　　　　(page 16)

2014		Folio	$
Dec. 28	Sales	SB 30	51,000

General Ledger

Sales Accounts　　　　　　(Page 124)

			2014		Folio	$
			Dec.31	Credit sales for the Month	SB30	117,500

Note: The credit sales for the month can also be called accounts receivable.

5.4 Purchase Invoices, Purchases Day Book and Ledgers

The information in the purchase invoices is posted to purchases day book or purchases journal. A **purchase Invoice** contains only credit purchases. All the purchases in the purchase invoices will be recorded in the **Purchases Day Book** and information in the purchases day book will be posted to **Purchases ledger** and **general ledger**.

Assume that the following source documents (purchases invoices) are collected by Samotex Ltd. (the buyer) from its suppliers:

Exhibit 5.4a

ASACOM Ltd.

No. 10, Victoria Island, Lagos, Nig.

Purchase Invoice

Your Purchase Order:12/B/120
Invoice No. 333
2 December, 2014

To:
Samotex Ltd.
No. 5, Obasa, Oyo Rd., Ib.
Nig.

	Unit Price $	Qty	Total $
Bags of Wheat	1,000	3	3,000
Bags of Rice	7,000	4	28,000
Bags of Semo	2,000	3	6,000
Total			37,000

Amounts in words: Thirty seven thousand dollars only.

Customer's Signature	Supplier's Signature
Samotex Ltd	ASACOM Ltd.

Exhibit 5.4b

PYZ Ltd
45 Charles Street
Manchester MI 5ZN

Purchase Invoice

Your Purchase Order: 12/p/121
Invoice No. 421
December 2, 2014

To:
Samotex
No. 5, Obasa, Oyo Rd. Ib. Nig.

	Unit Price $	Qty	Total $
Sachets of Spagetti	80	30	2,400
Packets of indomies	1,000	4	4,000
Bags of Semo	1,500	8	12,000
Total			18,400

Amounts in words: Eighteen thousand and four hundred dollars only.

Customer's Signature	Supplier's Signature
Samotex	PYZ Ltd

Exhibit 5.4c

ASACOM Ltd.

No. 10, Victoria Island, Lagos, Nig.

Purchase Invoice

Your Purchase Order:12/B/232
Invoice No. 253
6 December, 2014

To:
Samotex
No. 5, Obasa, Oyo Rd. Ib., Nig.
Oluyole,Ib. Nig

	Unit Price ($)	Q-y	Total($)
Bags of Wheat	2,000	3	6,000

Amounts in words: Six thousand dollars only.

Customer's Signature	Supplier's Signature
Samotex Ltd	ASACOM Ltd

Exhibit 5.4d

```
Jasper & Co.
No. 25, Victoria Island, Lagos, Nig
                    Purchase Invoice

Your purchase Order:13/B/122
Invoice No. 129
9 December, 2014


To:
Samotex Ltd
No. 5, Adeyemo,
Oluyole,Ib. Nig

                        Unit
                        Price($)   Qty   Total($)
    Bags of Wheat         1000     30    30,000
    Less 10% trade discount               -3,000
                                          27,000



Amounts in words: Twenty seven thousand dollars only.
Customer's Signature              Supplier's Signature
Samotex Ltd.                         Jasper & Co.
```

Purchases day book of Samotex Ltd

	Purchases Day Book			(page 29)
Date	Names	Invoice No.	Folio	Amount
2014				$
Dec.2	ASACOM Ltd.	333	PL18	37,000
Dec. 2	PYZ Ltd.	421	PL19	18,400
Dec. 6	ASACOM Ltd.	253	PL 18	6,000
Dec. 9	Jasper & Co.	129	PL22	27,000
Transfer to Purchases Account			GL122	88,400

Purchases ledger

ASACOMPU Ltd.   (Page 18)

2014	$	2014	Folio	$
		Dec. 2 Purchases	PB29	37,000
		Dec. 6 Purchases	PB29	6,000

PYZ Ltd.   (Page19)

2014	$	2014	Folio	$
		Dec. 2 Purchases	PB 29	18,400

Jasper & Co.   (Page 22)

2014	$	2014	Folio	$
		Dec. 9 Purchases	PB29	27,000

General Ledger

Purchases Accounts   (Page 122)

2014	Folio	$	2C14	$
Dec. 31 Credit purchases for the year	PB29	88,400		

5.5 Credit Notes, Returns Inwards Day Book and Ledgers

The information in the credit note will be recorded in the return inward day book, and the information in the return inward day book will be transferred to return inward ledger, and general ledger.

Assume that Samotex Ltd. issued the following source documents (credit notes) to its customers that returned some of the goods purchased.

Exhibit 5.5a

Credit Note

Samotex Ltd

No. 5, Obasa, Oyo Rd., Ib. Nig.

Date: 15/12/14

Credit Note No.: 121

To:
A. Adekunle
No. 10, Adeyemo,
Oluyole,Ib. Nig

	Unit Price $	Qty	Total $
Bag of Wheat	2,000	1	2,000

Amount in words: Two thousand dollars only.

Customer's Signature	Supplier's Signature
A. Adekunle	Samotex

Exhibit 5.5b

Credit Note

Samotex Ltd
No. 5, Obasa, Oyo Rd., Ib. Nig.

Credit Note No.: 122

15 December, 2014

To:
P. Smith
No. 10, Aluko,
Oluyole,Ib. Nig

	Unit Price $	Qty	Total $
Sachets of Spagetti	100	10	1,000

Amounts in words: One thousand dollars only.

Customer's Signature	Supplier's Signature
P. Smith	Samotex

Returns Inwards Day Book   (Page 16)

Date	Names	Credit Note Number	Folio	Amount
2014				$
Dec. 15	A. Adekunle	121	SL 4	2,000
Dec. 15	P. Smith	122	SL 6	1,000
Transfer to sales account			GL124	3,000

Sales Ledger

Dr.   Cr.

A. Adekunle Account   (Page 4)

		Folio	$
2014			
Dec.	Returns		
15	Inward	RI 16	2,000

Dr.   P. Smith Account (Page 6)   Cr.

		Folio	$
2014			
Dec.	Returns		
15	Inward	RI 16	1,000

General Ledger

Dr.   Returns Inwards Accounts   page (124)   Cr.

2014		Folio	$	
Dec. 31	Returns for	RI 16	3,000	
	the month			

5.6. Debit Note, Returns Outwards Day Book and the ledgers

Exhibit 5.6a

ASACOM Ltd.

No. 10, Victoria Island, Lagos, Nig.

Debit Note

Debit Note No. 221

7 December, 2014

To:
Samotex
No. 5, Obasa, Oyo Rd. Ib., Nig.
Oluyole,Ib. Nig

	Unit Price ($)	Qty	Total($)
Bags of Wheat	2,000	1	2,000

Amounts in words: Two thousand dollars only.

Customer's Signature	Supplier's Signature
Samotex Ltd	ASACOM Ltd

Exhibit 5.6b

Jasper & Co.

No. 25, Victoria Island, Lagos, Nig

Debit Note

Debit Note No. 129
December 12, 2014

To:
Samotex Ltd
No. 5, Adeyemo,
Oluyole,Ib. Nig

	Unit Price($)	Qty	Total($)
Bags of Wheat	1000	3	3,000
Less 10% trade discount			-300
			2,700

Amounts in words: Two thousand and seven hundred dollars only.

Customer's Signature	Supplier's Signature
Samotex Ltd.	Jasper & Co.

Returns Outwards Day Book   (page 24)

Date	Names	Debit Note Number	Folio	Amount
2014				$
Dec. 7	ASACOMPU	221	PL 6	2,000
Dec. 12	Jasper & Co	129	PL10	2,700

Transfer to sales account   GL12   4,700

Purchases Ledger

ASACOMPU Account   (Page 6)

Date 2014		Folio	$	
Dec. 7	Return outward	RO24	2,000	

Jasper & Co   (Page 10)

Date 2014		Folio	$	
Dec. 12	Return outward	RO24	2,700	

General ledger
Return Outward Accounts   (Page 12)

	Date 2014		Folio	$
	Dec. 31	Return outward for the month	RO24	4,700

CHAPTER 6

Cash Book

6.0.   Meaning of a Cash Book

A cash book is a journal in which all cash receipts and payments (including bank deposits and withdrawals are recorded initially, in chronological order, for posting to general ledger. It is established to exercise control over the movement of cash inflow and cash outflow of the business. A cash book balance is regularly reconciled with a bank statement balance as an internal audit measure. As the name suggests, only cash and bank transactions are recorded in the cash book.

A cash book may be referred to as a ledger or a journal (book of original entry). It is normally divided into two parts. The debit side and credit side.

6.0.1. Cash Receipt and payment

Cash collected or received by the business is entered on the debit side while cash paid out of the business is entered on the credit side.

6.0.2. Payment to Bank and Receipt from bank

Check received from a customer by the business and deposited into the bank will be entered on the debited side of a cash book (bank column only). Direct payment to the bank by customers will be debited to a cash book (bank column). Cash deposited into a bank account is debited to the cash book (bank column)

Check issued out and any other payment effected through the bank will be entered on the credit side of the cash book (bank column only). Cash withdrawn from the bank account will be credited to the cash book (bank column).

6.1. Contra Entries

Sometimes cash could be taken from an office to a bank, and cash could be withdrawn from the bank for the office use. When this happens, we have a situation called cross or contra entries. A contra entry is denoted by (c).

Example

Assume that on July 8, a business withdraws $600 from the bank for business use.

You are required to record the above in a cash book.

SOLUTION

Cash Book

Date	Particulars	Folio	Cash	Bank	Date	Particulars	Folio	Cash	Bank
July			$	$	July			$	$
8	Bank (c)		600		8	Cash (c)			600

Note: The above cash book is an example of two-column cash book.

6.2. Recording into Cash Book

Information in the source documents such as cash receipts, payment voucher, checks received, checks issued, credit card payments, and etc., are recorded in the cash book.

It has already been explained in the previous chapters of this book that recording in accounting books is based on the rule of double entry principles.

The rule states that for every debit entry there must be a corresponding credit entry and for every credit entry there must be a corresponding debit entry. It means that in a business, an account (ledger) must be open for the receiver, and another account must be open for the giver. As we have learned that cash book can be referred to as a ledger and as well as a book of original entry. In this context, we shall regard cash book as a ledger. It means that all transactions recorded in the cash book will be recorded in another ledger to complete the other leg of a double entry principle. Contra entry will not pass through the rule of a double entry because it has already been recorded twice within the cash book, and as a result of this it shall not be recorded on the other ledger to complete the double entry principles.

6.3. Cash Book and Other Ledgers

Items on the debit side of the cash book will be posted to the credit side of the affected ledger while items on the credit side of the cash book will be posted to the debit side of the concerned ledger. In order to avoid error, cash book should be prepared monthly.

6.4. Types of Cash Book

There are different types of cash book in use today. They are as follows:

1. One-Column Cash Book
2. Two- Column Cash Book
3. Three- Column Cash Book
4. Petty Cash Book

6.4.1. One-Column Cash Book

One-Column Cash Book: This could be a cash account or bank account controlling cash received or cash paid. It is a cash movement.

It could be cash account containing only cash transactions such as cash received from sales revenue, and income received for services rendered or cash paid for expenses. It could be bank account containing only bank transactions such as check received and check paid. It can also be called a single column cash book.

ILLUSTRATION 1

Enter the transaction below in a cash account of Mr. Jones, and balance off the accounts (close the ledgers) at the end of July 31, 2015.

July 1 cash balance at start $2,000
July 3 bought goods $1,200 in cash
July 5 received $400 from debtors in cash
July 8 paid wages $500 cash
July10 Cash sales $1,000
July 12 cash drawings $1,300

SOLUTION

Mr. Jones One-column Cash Book (Cash account)

Date		$	Date		$
2015			2015		
July 1	Balance b/f	2,000	July 3	Purchases	1,200
July 5	Debtors	400	July 8	Wages	500
July 10	Sales	1,000	July 12	Drawings	1,300
			July 31	Balance c/d	400
		3,400			3,400
August 1	Balance b/d	400			

ILLUSTRATION 2

The following transactions were extracted from the books of P. James. Enter the transactions in a bank account of Mr. P. James and balance off the accounts at the end of June 30, 2015.

June 1   Debit balance in bank at start $30,000
June 2   Paid into the bank additional cash $10,000
June 3   Bought goods for resale and paid by check $14,000
June 8   Received a check of $16,000 from debtors
June 10   Paid rent $4,000 by check

SOLUTION

P. James Single Column Cash Book (Bank Account)

Date		$	Date		$
2015			2015		
June 1	Balance b/f	30,000	June 3	Purchases	14,000
June 2	Cash	10,000	June 10	Rent	4,000
June 8	Debtors	16,000	June 30	Balance c/d	38,000
		56,000			56,000
July 1	Balance b/d	38,000			

Use of Folio Column

The detail column in an account is the name of the other leg of double entry of the account. It is easy to find the other account of the double entry by mere looking at the detail column provided the books kept are not many. However, when many books are being kept, mentioning the name of the first entry (first account) may not be sufficient information to find the second entry of the double entry (other account) quickly. More information about the location of the other account is needed. This is given by the folio column.
A folio column is added to each account, and each book at their extreme right corner for easy reference of the other account or book. In the column, the name of the other book and the number of the page in the other book where the other part of the double entry is recorded will be stated against each and every entry.

In order to ensure that the double entry is complete, the folio column should only be filled in when the double entry has been completed.

Example

An entry for payment of cash into T. Jones' account whose account was on page 12 of the purchase ledger, and the cash recorded on page 29 of the cash book, would have the following folio column entries:

In the cash book; the folio column entry would be PL 12

In the Purchases Ledger; the folio column entry would be CB29

Where:
PL = Purchases Ledger
CB= cash Book

6.4.2. Two-Column Cash Book

Two-column cash book has both cash and bank columns together on either side of a ledger account. All the cash transactions will be recorded under cash column while all bank transactions will be recorded under bank column. At the end of the period, there will be cash and bank balances.

ILLUSTRATION

The following transactions were extracted from the source documents of Jane enterprises, within the month of July, 2015. Record the transactions in the two-column cash book of Jane enterprises and balance off the account as on July 31, 2015.

July 1	Started business with $1,000 cash
July 2	paid wages of $400 in cash
July 3	bought goods $500 by check
July 8	withdrew $600 for business use
July 10	cash sales $800 paid direct into bank
July 12	bought goods for $650 on credit

SOLUTION

Jane Two-Column Cash Book   Page 88

Date	Particulars	Folio	Cash	Bank	Date	Particulars	Folio	Cash	Bank
2015 July			$	$	2015 July			$	$
	Capital	PrL10	1,000						
8	Bank (c)		600		2	Wages	GL28	400	
10	Sales	GL32		800	3	Purchases	PL 30		500
					8	Cash (c)			600
	Balance c/d			300	31	Balance c/d		1,200	
			1,600	1,100				1,600	1,100
Aug.1	Balance b/d		1,200		Aug.1	Balance b/d			300

Note:
PrL = Private Ledger
GL = General Ledger
PL = Purchases Ledger

Cash Discounts

Cash Discount is the amount of reduction in the price of goods sold to a customer as a result of prompt payment. It is an allowance given to a customer for quick payment. It is used to encourage prompt payment.

It can be stated in an absolute value or in a percentage. If it is stated in percentage, the (rate) percentage will be used to multiply the sales value of the goods; the result obtained is the cash discount. Cash discount can either be paid by cash or check.

A business may have two types of cash discounts in its books. They are:

1) Discount received: This is a cash discount received by a business from its suppliers when it pays what it owes them promptly.

2) Discount allowed: This is a cash discount given by a business to its customers when they pay their accounts quickly.

6.4.3 Three -Column Cash Book

It is important to avoid too many entries in the general ledger. As a result of this, two columns for cash discounts are included in the cash book. There is a column for discount allowed on the debit side and discount received on the credit side of the cash book. Only total of each of the column would be recorded in the ledger.

Why is a discount allowed debited, and a discount received credited?

The reasons are as follows:

1) Discount allowed is an expense, and every item that increases expense should be debited in the book of accounts
2) Discount received is an income, and every item that increases income should be credited in the book of account

Examples

The following examples demonstrate the effects of cash discounts in books of accounts of our business:

Example 1

P. James owed us $200. He pays us in cash on May 1, 2014 which is within the time limit applicable for a 10 per cent cash discount. He pays $200 - $20 = $180 in full settlement of his account.

	Effect	Action
1.	Cash entry	
a.	Asset (cash) is increased by $180.	Debit cash account(record $180 to the debit column of Cash book)
b.	Asset (account receivable) is decreased by $180	Credit P. Jones $180
2.	Discount allowed	
a.	Expense (Discount allowed) is increased by $20	Debit Discount allowed account $20
b.	Asset (account receivable) is decreased by $20. $20 being discount allowed to P. Jones.	Credit P. Jones account $20.

Example 2

The business owed S. Steven $9,000. We pay him by check on May 5, 2014 which is within the time limit laid down by him for $2 1/2$ percent cash discount. The business will pay $9,000 - $225 = $8,775 in full settlement of the account.

	Effect	Action
1.	Check	
a.	Asset (bank) is reduced by $8,775.	Credit bank (record $8,775 to the credit side of bank column)
b.	Liability (account payable) is reduced by $8,775	Debit S. Steven account $8,775
2.	Discount Received	
a.	Income (Discount received) is increased by $225	Credit Discount received account $225
b.	Liability (account payable) is decreased by $225. $225 being discount received from S. Steven	Debit account payable account (S. Steven account $225)

Our Business Cash Book   (Page 52)
Three -Column Cash Book

Date	Particulars	Folio	Disc	Cash	Bank	Date	Particulars	Folio	Disc	Cash	Bank
2014			$	$	$	2014			$	$	$
May						May					
1	P. James	SL30	20	180		5	S. Steven	PL26	225		8,775

General Ledgers

Dr.   **Cr.**

Discount Allowed Account   (General Ledger 15)

Date		Folio	$	Date		Folio	$
2014				2014			
May 1	P. James	CB52	20				

Dr.   **Cr.**

Discount Received Account   (General Ledger 16)

Date		Folio	$	Date		Folio	$
2014				2014			
				May 5	S. Steven	CB52	225

Sales Ledger

P. James Account   (Sales Ledger 30)

Date		Folio	$	Date		Folio	$
2014				2014			
May 1	Balance	b/f	200	May 1	Cash	CB52	180
				May 1	Discount	CB52	20
			200				200

Purchases Ledger

S. Steven Accounts   Purchases Ledger 26

Date		Folio	$	Date		Folio	$
2014				2014			
May 5	Discount	CB52	225	May 1	Balance	b/f	9,000
May 5	Bank	CB52	8,775				
			9,000				9,000

ILLUSTRATION

The following were extracted from the books of Steven Enterprises:

2013	$
March 1	
Cash balance	58
Bank balance	1,308
Accounts receivable accounts:	
B. Popson	240
N. Smith	560
D. Jasper	80
Account Payable:	
U. Adams	120
A. Alice	880
R. Barrack	200

March 2 B. Popson pays us by check, having deducted 2 1/2 percent cash discount ($6); $234.

March 8, we paid R. Barrack his account by check deducting 5 percent cash discount ($10); $190.

March 11, we withdrew $200 cash from the bank for business use; $200.

March 16. N. Smith pays us his account by check deducting 2 1/2 percent cash discount ($14); $546.

March 25, we paid office expenses in cash; $184

March 28, D. Jasper pays us in cash after having deducted 5 percent cash discount ($4); $76

March 29, we paid U. Adams by check less 5 percent cash discount ($6) ; 114

March 30, we pay A. Alice by check less 2 1/2 percent cash discount ($22); $858

SUGGESTED SOLUTION

Our Business
Three-Column Cash Book

Date	Particulars	Folio	Disc.	Cash	Bank	Date	Particulars	Folio	Disc.	Cash	Bank
2013			$	$	$	2013			$	$	$
Mar.						Mar.					
1	Balance	b/f		58	1,308	8	R. Barrack	PL25	10		190
2	B.Popson	SL20	6		234	11	Cash	(c)			200
11	Bank	(c)		200		25	office exp.	GL55		184	
16	N. Smith	SL22	14		546	29	U. Adams	PL29	6		114
28	D. Jasper	SL25	4	76		30	A. Alice	PL31	22		858
						31	Balance	c/d		150	726
			24	334	2,088				38	334	2,088
Apr. 1	Balance	b/d		150	726						

Sales ledger
B. Popson — (Sales ledger page 20)

Date		Folio	$	Date		Folio	$
2013				2013			
Mar.1	Balance	b/f	240	Mar. 2	Bank	CB11	234
				Mar. 2	Discount	CB11	6
			240				240

N. Smith — (Sales ledger page 22)

Date		Folio	$	Date		Folio	$
2013				2013			
Mar.1	Balance	b/f	560	Mar. 16	Bank	CB11	546
				Mar. 16	Discount	CB11	14
			560				560

A. Jasper Account (Sales ledger page 25)

Date		Folio	$	Date		Folio	$
2013				2013			
Mar.1	Balance	b/f	80	Mar. 28	Cash	CB11	76
				Mar. 28	Discount	CB11	4
			80				80

Purchases Ledger

R. Barrack   (Purchases ledger page 25)

Date		Folio	$	Date		Folio	$
2013				2013			
Mar. 8	Bank	CB11	190	Mar.1	Balance	b/f	200
Mar. 8	Discount	CB11	10				
			200				200

U. Adams   (Purchases Ledger 29)

Date		Folio	$	Date		Folio	$
2013				2013			
Mar. 29	Bank	CB11	114	Mar. 1	Balance	b/f	120
Mar. 29	Discount	CB11	6				
			120				120

A. Alice   (Purchases Ledger page 31)

Date		Folio	$	Date		Folio	$
2013				2013			
Mar. 30	Bank	CB11	858	Mar.1	Balance	b/f	880
May. 30	Discount	CB11	22				
			880				880

General Ledger

Office Expenses   (General Ledger page 66)

Date		Folio	$	Date	Folio	$
2013				2013		
Mar. 25	Cash	CB11	184			

Discount Allowed   (General Ledger page 66)

Date		Folio	$	Date	Folio	$
2013				2013		
Mar. 31	Total for the Month	CB11	24			

Discount Received   (General Ledger Page 70)

Date	Folio	$	Date		Folio	$
2013			2013			
			Mar. 31	Total for the Month	CB11	38

Bank Overdrafts

The balance in the bank account is often a debit balance. There are some exceptional situations where a company can borrow money from a bank by a way of bank overdrafts. This means that a company may withdraw or pay more than its bank balance (the money it has in the bank account). When there are bank overdrafts, the bank balance will no longer be a debit balance but a credit balance.

6.4.4 Petty Cash Book

Any small amount of money held by a responsible officer for meeting duly authorized small expenses is called a petty cash. The method of keeping petty cash is called imprest system.

When an imprest system is in operation with the petty cash book, a float is established to meet the petty cash payments. At the end of the month, the total amount spent is reimbursed. At any given time, the amount on the paid vouchers and the cash in the hand of the petty cashier should be equal to the amount of the float.

CHAPTER 7

CAPITAL EXPENDITURE AND REVENUE EXPENDITURE

Capital expenditure and revenue expenditure have been sources of confusion for many students and business owners. It is necessary to distinguish between the two vividly.

7.1. Capital expenditure

The first thing you need to understand is that a capital expenditure is totally different from capital that is contributed by the owner of the business. Capital expenditure is different from capital (owner's equity). Capital is the fund invested in the business by the owner of the business.

Capital expenditure is incurred during the course of the business to acquire non-current assets or to increase the value of existing non-current assets. It does not appear in statement of comprehensive income (profit and loss accounts). It appears in a statement of financial position (balance sheet) alone. Examples of capital expenditures are:

1) Acquisition of non- current assets
2) The cost of bringing the assets into the business premises
3) Installation cost
4) The legal cost of buying buildings
5) Cost of putting the non-current assets into use.
6) Import duty paid on importing non-current asset

7.2. Revenue expenditure

Revenue expenditure can be defined as a routine expenditure of a business. It is not the cost incurred on the acquisition of non- current assets or cost of increasing the value of non- current asset.

Differences between capital expenditure and revenue expenditure can be explained further by the table below:

Details of Expenditures	Types of Expenditures
Fuel cost	Revenue
Expansion of business premises	Capital
Cost of renovating office	Revenue
Buying vehicle	Capital
Repair of vehicle	Revenue
Electricity cost	Revenue
Replacing parts of machinery	Revenue
Increasing capacity of machinery	Capital

It has already been mentioned that capital expenditure should be treated in a statement of financial position, and revenue expenditure should be treated in the statement of comprehensive income. Efforts should be made not to intermingle the posting of the above mentioned transactions in the books of account in order to avoid costly errors. If there are joint expenditures that combine both capital expenditures and revenue expenditures, the expenditures need to be separated before posting.

7. 3 Capital receipts

The sale of an item of capital expenditure is classified as capital receipt. For example, machinery that costs $15,000 was sold for $1,500 after 4years. $15,000 was treated as capital expenditure, while $1,500 received is treated as capital receipt and credited to machinery disposal accounts in the general ledger account.

7.4 Revenue receipts

Revenue receipts are all the revenue and other income that are added to gross profit to get total income. Examples are discount received and commissions receivable.

ILLUSTRATION 1

Mr. Femi, a farmer bought a tractor and 10 cutlasses for $450,000 and $850 respectively. He incurred the following expenses for the year ended 31st December, 2012.

Wages	$69,000
Yam tuba	$11,000
Maize	$2,000

He received $4,900 from customers. The tractor was later sold for $250,000. Compute the following:

a) Capital Expenditure

b) Revenue Expenditure

c) Revenue Receipts

d) Capital Receipts

Solution

a) Capital Expenditure

	$
Tractor	450,000
Cutlasses	850
Capital Expenditure	450,850

b) Revenue Expenditure

	$
Wages	69,000
Yam tuba	11,000
Maize	2,000
Revenue Expenditure	82,000

c) Revenue Receipts

Amount received from customers is his revenue receipts.
Revenue Receipts = $4,900

    d) Capital Receipts
The amount at which the tractor was sold is his capital receipts.

Capital Receipts = $250,000

CHAPTER 8

BAD DEBTS AND ALLOWANCES FOR DOUBTFUL DEBTS

8.1. Bad debts

Credit sales cannot be totally eradicated in business. It forms a larger volume of sales made by many companies. There is a probability that some of the customers may not pay for the goods purchased on credit. The business entity, therefore, suffers the risk of default.

The default is called bad debts in accounting. It is classified as a normal business expense. It should be charged to an income statement as an expense for the period. It should also be deducted from asset accounts (**Accounts Receivable**).

To record a bad debt; debit it to bad debt account so as to increase expense account, and credit it to debtors' account (accounts receivable) to reduce the debt or eradicate the debt.

There are different probable circumstances that may exist concerning a bad debt. They are as follows:

1) The debtor died or go bankrupt; it is inevitable that nothing can be received.

2) The debtor indicates that only part of the total amount due on the invoice will be paid by him.

The above two statements can be illustrated below:

1) The debtor (T.Jev) died or go bankrupt; it is inevitable that nothing can be received.

T. Jev
Accounts

2010		$	2010			$
			Dec.			
Mar. 1	Sales	400	31		Bad debt	400

2) The debtor (B. Blazer) indicates that only part of the total amount due on the invoice will be paid by him.

B. Blazer Accounts

2010		$	2010		$
			Sept.		
Jan. 3	Sales	500	18	Bank	350
				Bad	
			Dec.31	debt	150
		500			500

	Bad debts		
2010	$	2010	$
Dec. 31 T. Jev	400	Dec. 31 P&L	550
Dec. 31 B. Blazer	150		
	550		550

An extract of income statement (P&L) for the year ended 31 December 2010.

	$
Gross Profit	XX
Less Expenses: Bad debts	(550)

8.2. ALLOWANCE FOR DOUBTFUL DEBTS

Death and bankruptcy may make it infeasible for debtors to pay their debts. It means that the amounts owed by debtors become irrecoverable and shall be treated as a trading loss for the period under consideration.

In a situation where the decease's customer leaves an estate, the estate shall contribute to the recovery of the debts. The difference between the total debts owed by the deceased debtor and the amount the estate is able to contribute shall be considered as bad debts.

The main aim of allowance for doubtful debts is to record accounts receivable in the statement of financial position at a realistic value. The estimation of how probable and likely a debt will be bad is called allowance for doubtful debt or provision for doubtful debt.

It is difficult to determine with certainty at the end of a year the true amount of debts that will not be paid by debtors. How do you decide on the allowance? For the purpose of arriving at a figure for allowance for doubtful debt, a business entity must first consider that some debtors will not pay any of their debts, while some will pay only a portion of the amount owing, leaving the remainder permanently unpaid.

The estimate figure can be determined in the following ways:

1. by looking at individual debt, and deciding to what extent it will be bad;
2. by estimating on the basis of past experience, what percentage of the total debts remaining unpaid will finally prove to be bad debts.

It is generally believed that the longer a debt is being owed, the more likely it is going to be bad debt.
Some business entities prepare an "ageing schedule" showing how long a debt has been remained unpaid.

Older debtors should be assigned higher percentage estimate than newer debtors.

DEBTORS AGEING SCHEDULE

Period of debt	Amount	Estimate percentage of doubtful debts	Allowance for doubtful debts
	$	%	
Less than 1 Month	2,500	2	50
1 Month to 3	1,500	4	60

months			
3 months to 5 months	1,000	5	50
5 months to 1 year	600	6	36
over 1 year	160	15	24
	5,760		220

8.2.1. Increase in Allowance for Doubtful Debts

 Where an allowance for doubtful debt in the current year is higher than the allowance for doubtful debt in the previous year, the difference should be charged to the income statement (Profit and Loss Accounts). The amount reduces a profit.

The formulas for the computation of allowances for doubtful debt for each period are as follows:

 Opening allowance for doubtful debts =Opening accounts receivable × rate of allowance for doubtful debt

Closing allowance for doubtful debts =Closing accounts receivable × rate of allowance for doubtful debt

Closing allowance for doubtful debt should be posted to a statement of financial position as a deduction from the accounts receivable for the current year. The following illustration can be used to explain it further.

ILLUSTRATION 1

The following were extracted from the books of Jando as at 31st Dec. 2013.
Accounts receivable brought forward from the previous year is $20,000. Accounts receivable for the current year is $24,000. You are given that the rate of allowance for doubtful debts is 2%. You are

required to record the above transactions in the books of accounts.

Solution:

1) Debit profit and loss account
2) Credit allowance for doubtful debt accounts

Allowance for Doubtful Debts Accounts

2013		$	2013		$
			Jan. 1	Balance b/f	400
Dec. 31	Balance	480		P & L	80
		480			480
			Jan.1 2014	Balance b/d	480

Profit and Loss Accounts

2013	$	2013	$
Allowance for doubtful debts	80		

Statement of Comprehensive income for the year eneded 31st Dec.,2013

Gross Profit	XX
Less allowance for doubtful debts	-80

Statement of Financial Position as at 31st Dec., 2013

	$	$
Current Assets	24,000	
Less: allowance for		
doubtful debts	(480)	
	23,520	

NOTE:

2% is the rate of allowance for doubtful debt. It should be used to multiply account receivable for each period to get the allowance for doubtful debt for each period.

Workings:

Opening allowance for doubtful debts = $20,000 ×2% = $400

Closing allowance for doubtful debts = $24,000 × 2% = $480

8. 2. 2. Decrease in Allowance for Doubtful Debts

You need to do the opposite of what you did to the increase in allowance for doubtful debt, in order to decrease the allowance.

Where the accounts receivable in a current year is less than that of previous year, the allowance for doubtful debt in the current year will be less than the allowance for doubtful debt in the previous year and hence, the profit and loss account should be credited with the difference between allowances for doubtful debts.

Double entry bookkeeping for the records are:

      1) Debit Allowance for Doubtful Debts Accounts

      2) Credit income statements (Profit and Loss Accounts)

ILLUSTRATION 2

The following were extracted from the books of Smith Ltd as at 31St Dec. 2012.

Accounts receivable brought forward is $20,000. Accounts receivable as at 31St Dec.2012 is $17,000. You are given that the rate of the allowance is 2%. You are required to prepare the necessary accounts.

SOLUTION

Allowance for doubtful debts

2012		$	2012		$
	P & L	60	Jan. 1	Balance b/f	400
Dec. 31	Balance	340			
		400			400
			2013		

| | | Jan. 1 | Balance b/d | 340 |

Profit and Loss Accounts

2012	$	2012	$
		Allowance for doubtful debts	60

Statement of Comprehensive income for the year eneded 31st Dec.2012

	$
Gross Profit	XX
Add allowance for doubtful debts	60

Statement of financial position as at 31st December, 2012

	$	$
Current Assets:		
Accounts receivable	17,000	
Less allowance for doubtful debts	(340)	
	16,660	

ILLUSTRATION 3

Year to 31st	Debtors after bad debts written off	Allowance for doubtful debts
Dec.	$	$
1990	60,000	600
1991	65,000	650
1992	63,000	630

a)   What was the treatment of allowance for doubtful debts in the statement of comprehensive income (Profit and Loss Account) for 1991?

b) In 1992, debtors figure will appear in the balance sheet as

SOLUTION:

a) $50 should be debited to a statement of comprehensive income.

b) $63,000 – $630 = $62,370

ILLUSTRATION 4

The accounts receivable of a trading concern is $66,000. Out of this, 2% is irrecoverable;
5 percent of the balance is unlikely to be collected.

a) How much is the bad debt?

b) What is the allowance for doubtful debt?

Solution:

a. $66,000 \times 2\% = \$1,320$

b. $(66,000 - 1,320) \times 5\% = \$3,234$

ILLUSTRATION 5

Use the following information to answer questions a. & b.

Accounts Receivables as at	1/6/2013	$300,450
Accounts Receivables as at	31/5/2014	$525,110
Specific bad debts during the year		$41,000
Allowance for bad and doubtful debts as at 1/6/2013		$12,500

The provision for bad and doubtful debts is maintained at a level of 5% of accounts receivable as at 31/5/2014.

a. What is the value of Accounts Receivables that will be remaining as at 31/5/2014 in the statement of financial position (balance sheet)?

b. What is the amount of allowance for bad and doubtful debts to be recorded in a statement of comprehensive income (profit and loss accounts) for the year ended 31 May 2014?

SOLUTION:

a. The value of accounts receivable that will be remaining as at 31/5/2014 in the statement of financial position (balance sheet)

	$
Accounts receivable 31/5/2014	525,110
Less Bad debt for the year	(41,000)
	484,110
Allowance for doubtful debts(484,110×5%)	(24,206)
	459,904

The value of accounts receivable that will be remaining as at 31/5/2014 in the statement of financial position (balance sheet) is $459,904.

b. Allowance for bad and doubtful debts to be shown in the statements of comprehensive income (profit and loss accounts)

Allowance for bad and doubtful debts Accounts

		Balance b/d	12,500
Balance c/d	24,206	income (P&L)	11,706
	24206		24,206

The amount of allowance for bad and doubtful debts to be recorded (debited) in the statement of comprehensive income (profit and loss accounts) for the year ended 31 May 2014 is $11,706.

8.3. Bad Debts Recovered

Sometimes, a debt written off in previous years may be recovered.

The accounting entries for the above statement are:

1. Reinstate the debt by making the following entries:

Dr: Debtor's account

Cr: Bad debts recovered account

2. When payment is recovered from the debtor in settlement of all or part of the debt:

Dr: Cash/bank

Cr: Debtor's account

With the amount received.

At the end of the financial year, the credit balance in the bad debts recovered account is transferred either to the bad debts account or direct to the credit side of the profit and loss account at the end of the financial year.

CHAPTER 9

PREPAID EXPENSES AND ACCRUED EXPENSES

9.1 Prepaid Expenses

Prepaid expenses are the payment paid for services not yet enjoyed. They are also the expenditures which at the end of an accounting period have not been consumed. They constitute costs of future income. Only the portions of the costs actually consumed during an accounting period should be considered as an expense for that period. The amounts representing unconsumed costs should be carried forward to the next accounting period, as prepaid expenses in the statement of financial position as a current asset at the end of an accounting period.

For example, a Landlord collects $100 monthly from his tenant, at the end of the year, the tenant is expected to pay ($100 ×12) = $1,200 to his landlord as rent. But if the tenant paid $2,000, he has overpaid by $800. This $800 is the prepaid rent which is a current asset in the statement of financial position for the period. It is only $1,200 expected to be paid for the year that will appear in the statement of comprehensive income (profit and loss account) of the accounting period. In the future, the total rent he will pay the landlord will be less than $800.

Example 2

A landlord collects $250 monthly from his tenant, and the tenant has overpaid $400 in the previous year and during the year, he paid $3,200. What are the amount that will be considered in the statement of comprehensive income as an expense for the year, and the amount that will be shown as a current asset in the statement of financial position as at the year end?

Solution:

Rent A/C				
	$			$
Balance				
b/f	400	P&L		3,000
		Balance		
Cash	3,200	c/d		600
	3,600			3,600

The amount that will be recorded in the statement of comprehensive income as an expense for the year is $3,000 and the amount that will be shown as a current asset in the statement of financial position as at the year end is $600.

NOTE:
Prepaid expenses are the opposite of prepaid income.

9.2 Accrual or Accrued Expenses
Accrued expenses are the services enjoyed in the past, but payment is yet to be paid. Accrued expenses can also be defined

as expenses due but not yet paid for. The portion of the expenses remaining unpaid is called expenses owing or accrual.

Example 1

If wages of workers of a company are $2,000 per annum, and $1,800 were settled out of it. The amount owing the workers is $200. The $200 will be posted to a statement of financial position as a current liability (accrued expenses).

NOTE: Accrued expenses are the opposite of accrued income.

ILLUSTRATION

The illustration below consists of both prepaid and accrued expenses.

The trial balance extracted from the books of Mr. Timi as at December 31, 2006 included the following debit balances.

	$
Rent paid	2,000
Rates	1,500
Wages	72,500
Interest on loan	350

The following adjustments have to be made before the preparation of final accounts:

	31/12/2005	31/12/2006
	$	$
Rent outstanding	1,000	500
Rates paid in advance	500	600
Wages accrued	1,000	750

Interest on loan unpaid	1,200	1,400

(a) Show the amount of rates that will be debited to the statement of comprehensive Income (profit and loss accounts) for the year ended 31st December, 2006.

(b) What is the amount of rent that will be debited to profit and loss account for the year ended 31st Dec. 2006?

(c) What is the amount of interest on loan that will be recorded in the statement of financial position (balance sheet) and as what, as at 31st Dec. 2006?

(d) Show amount of wages that will appear on the statement of comprehensive income and statement of financial position respectively.

Solution:

(a)

Rates Accounts

	$			$
Balance b/d	500	P&L		1,400
Cash	1,500	Balance c/d		600
	2,000			2,000
Balance b/d	600			

The amount of rates that will be debited to the statement of comprehensive Income (profit and loss accounts) for the year ended 31st December, 2006 is $1,400.

(b)

Rent Accounts			
	$		$
Cash	2,000	Balance b/d	1,000
Balance c/d	500	P&L	1,500
	2,500		2,500
		Balance c/d	500

The amount of rent that will be debited to profit and loss account for the year ended 31st Dec. 2006 is $1,500.

(c)

Interest on loan Accounts			
	$		$
Cash	350	Balance b/d	1,200
Balance c/d	1,400	P&L	550
	1750		1,750
		Balance b/d	1,400

The amount of interest on a loan that will be recorded in the statement of financial position (balance sheet) as 31st Dec. 2006 is $1,400, and as a current liability.

(d)

Wages Accounts			
	$		$
Cash	72,500	Bal b/d	1,000
Balance c/d	750	P&L	72,250
	73,250		73,250
		Balance b/d	750

The amount of wages that will appear on the statement of comprehensive income is $72,250 and statement of financial position is $750.

CHAPTER 10

DEPRECIATION OF NON-CURRENT ASSETS

10.0 **Depreciation**

Depreciation is the part of a non-current asset that is consumed during its period of use by the business.

IAS 16 describes depreciation as,

"Both the decline in value of an asset over time as well as the systematic allocation of the depreciable amount of an asset over its useful life."

Depreciation is an expense. It needs to be charged to the statement of comprehensive income (Profit and Loss account) as an expense. The depreciation charged to income statement is called depreciation expense. The amount charged in a year for depreciation will be determined based on the amount of economic usefulness of the asset.

Total depreciation over the life of a non-current asset can be calculated simply as cost less the amount receivable when the non-current asset is put out of use by a business entity. This amount receivable is commonly referred to as scrap value or residual value of the asset.

Residual value can be determined based on the current market prices of the asset as at the day of the financial position, and not at the day of original purchase of the asset.

Where a non-current asset is sold within the same accounting period at a price lower than its cost of acquisition, the difference should be charged to the income statement as a provision for depreciation for the period. For example, a non-current asset that was bought for

$950, was sold for $450 in the same accounting year. The depreciation to be charged to an income statement for the year will be $950 – 450 =$500

Where a non-current asset is used for more than one accounting period, depreciation should be charged for each accounting period. How then do you allocate depreciation to each accounting period? There are many methods for the calculation and allocation of depreciation. The methods may not give the same result. It is important that it is shared over the useful life of each asset.

Non-Current Assets Held for Sale

Where non-current assets are regrouped as being non-current assets held for sales, depreciation must not be provided for the assets.

10.1 Causes of Depreciation

Reduction in the value of tangible non-current assets can arise as a result of physical deterioration, economic factors, time and depletion. The following are the causes of depreciation:

Physical deterioration

a) Wear and Tear: When non-current assets such as plant and machinery, fixtures and fittings are being used, they will eventually wear out.

b) Rust, erosion, decay and rot: metal in machinery will rust away. Wood rots.

Economic Factors

This may be the cause of an asset not to be put to use despite the fact that the asset is still in good condition and quality. Economic factors can occur in different ways such as obsolescence and inadequacy.

1) Obsolescence: It occurs when an asset is out of date as a result of advancement in technology.

2) Inadequacy: This occurs when an asset is abandoned as a result of its inability to cope with the expansion and growth of the business. This does not mean that the asset is no longer in good condition. For example, a small grinding machine used for producing animal feeds will be inadequate if the business of the animal feeds becomes very big.

Depletion

Some assets are of wasting nature, probably due to extraction of mineral resources or raw materials from them. Natural resources such as oil well, queries and mines come under this heading. Provision for the consumption of an asset of wasting nature is called provision for depletion.

Reason for Charging Depreciation

1. To know the actual net profit for the period
2. To comply with the matching concepts
3. To know the realistic value of the assets on the statements of financial position
4. To provide funds for assets replacement

10.2 Methods of calculating depreciation charges

There are many methods of calculating depreciation. Some of them are stated below:

1. Straight-line method
2. Diminishing or reducing balance method
3. Sum of the years' digit method

4. Annuity system
5. Sinking fund method
6. Insurance policy system
7. Revaluation method
8. Production unit method
9. Machine Hours method
10. Depreciation fund method

10.3. How to Calculate Depreciation of Non-Current Asset Based on IFRS

IAS 16 states that,

"The depreciation method should reflect the pattern in which the asset's future economic benefits are expected to be consumed by a business entity and that appropriateness of the method should be reviewed at least annually in case there has been a change in the expected pattern."

Beyond that, the standard leaves the choice of method to the entity, even though it does cite 'straight-line', 'diminishing balance', and 'units of production' methods.

There are many methods in use for the calculation of depreciation. International Financial Reporting Standards (IFRS) recommends three methods for the calculation of depreciation. They are the straight line, the reducing balance method and the unit of production method.

10.3.1 Reducing Balance Method or Diminishing Balance Method

In this method, a fixed percentage of the cost/balance of the asset is deducted from the cost in the first year, in the second year and subsequent years; the fixed percentage will be deducted from each reduced balance.

Reducing balance method can also be referred to as diminishing balance method.

Illustration 1

If a machine is bought for $20,000 and depreciation is to be charged at 20 per cent, the calculations for the first three years would be as follows:

Solution:

Reducing balance method

		$
Cost		20,000
Less first year depreciation	(20% × 20,000)	-4,000
		16,000
Second year depreciation	(20% × 16,000)	-3,200
		12,800
Third year depreciation	(20% ×12,800)	-2,560
Cost not yet apportioned at end of year 3		10,240

Depreciation using a diminishing balance method can also be calculated by a formula.

$$R = [1- \sqrt[n]{s/c}\ ] \times 100\%$$

Where:

R = the required rate per cent

n = number of years

s = scrap value

c = cost of the asset

ILLUSTRATION

Machinery is bought for $20,000. Its life is estimated to be six years, and its break-up value at the end of the period is $3,560.

Required:

    a) Determine the rate of depreciation per year

    b) Show depreciation for each year up to year six

SOLUTION

a)

$R = [1 - \sqrt[n]{s/c}] \times 100\%$

$\quad = [1 - \sqrt[6]{\$3,560/\$20,000}] \times 100\%$

$= [1 - \sqrt[6]{0.178}] \times 100\%$

$= 24.9985 \times 100\%$

$= 25\%$

The rate of depreciation per year is 25%.

b) The calculated rate of depreciation is applied to each year as follows:

	$
Cost in Year 1	20,000
Depreciation in year 1 (20,000 × 25%)	-5,000
	15,000
Depreciation in year 2 (15,000 ×25%)	-3,750
	11,250
Depreciation in year 3 (11,250 × 25%)	-2,813
	8,437

Depreciation in year 4 (8,437 × 25%)	-2,109
	6,328
Depreciation in year 5 (6,328 × 25%)	-1,582
	4,746
Depreciation in year 6 (4,746 × 25%)	-1,187
Scrap value	3,559

The scrap or break-up value is $3,560 approximately. $3,560 is the book value of the asset at the end of year six.

10.3.2 Straight Line Method

Under the straight line method of depreciation, the cost of acquisition of the asset should be identified. The number of years in which the asset will be put to use should also be known. The cost is then divided by the number of years. The result is the depreciation charged for each year.

Illustration 1

Machinery was purchased for $50,000 and we estimated that it will be put to use for 6 years and thereafter sold for $3,500. What is the depreciation charged for each year?

Solution:

$$\text{Depreciation} = \frac{\$50,000 - \$3,500}{6}$$

$$= \$7,750$$

On the other hand, if we believed that after 6years, the asset will not have a residual value, the charge for depreciation will be:

$$= \frac{\$50,000 - 0}{6}$$

$$= \$8,333.33$$

10.3.3 Units of Production Depreciation Methods

The units of production depreciation method is the most accurate and appropriate method of calculating depreciation, where the extent and amount of depreciation is determined by the usage of an asset during production.

Its use is limited to those assets for which some estimates of production can be attached, but it is a particular choice of those who use activity-based costing systems because it closely relates asset cost to actual activity.
    To calculate it, estimate the total amount of the expected units of production that can be produced by the asset.

Step1

Divide the cost of the assets after residual value (cost – residual value) by the expected total units of production to arrive at depreciation per unit.

Step 2

Multiply the depreciation per unit by the total units of production in a particular accounting period to arrive at the depreciation for the period.

ILLUSTRATION 1

A machine, at an oil company, is assembled at a cost of $700,000. It is expected to be used in the extraction of 2 million barrels of oil, which results in an anticipated depreciation rate of $0.35 per barrel. During the first month, 47,000 barrels of oil were extracted.

What is the depreciation for the period?

SOLUTION:

The depreciation for the month:

= Depreciation per unit of production × total production for the Period

= $0.35 × 47,000 barrels

= $16,450

This calculation also can be used with service hours as its basis rather than units of production. When used in this manner, the method can be applied to a larger number of assets for which production volumes would not be otherwise available.

10.3.4 Other Methods of Calculating Depreciation

The following are the other methods of calculating depreciation:

10.3.4.1 Depletion Unit Method

Depletion unit method should be used in calculating depreciation of non-current asset like quarry from which raw materials are dug out to be sold to the building industries.

If a quarry was bought for $10,000 and it was expected to contain 2,000 tons of saleable materials, then for each tons extracted, we would depreciate it by $5, since $10,000/2,000 = $5.

It can be shown below:

Cost of Assets/Expected total contents in units × (number of units taken in a period)

10.3.4.2 Machine Hour Method

Here the cost of machine will be divided by the total expected hours in the life of the machine and then multiply the result by the number of hours in which the machine is used in a period. A business which bought a machine costing $8,000 having an expected running life of 4,000 hours, and no scrap value, could provide for depreciation of the machine at the rate of $2 for every hour it was operated during a particular accounting period.

10.3.4.3 Sum of the Years' Digits Method

This is an alternative to diminishing balance method. It is commonly used in the US but not popular in the UK. It provides for higher depreciation to be charged early in the life of an asset and with lower depreciation in the later years.

ILLUSTRATION

Machinery is bought for $26,000. Its estimated life is 6 years and the residual value at the end of the sixth year is $5,000. You are required to show the depreciation for each year up to year six using sum of the years' digits method of depreciation.

Total depreciation = Cost – residual value

= $26,000 - $5,000

= $21,000

Sum of the digits = 1+2+3+4+5+6

= 21 years

Years		Annual Depreciation
		$
year 1	6/21 × $21,000	6,000
year 2	5/21 × $21,000	5,000
year 3	4/21 × $21,000	4,000
year 4	3/21 × $21,000	3,000
year 5	2/21 × $21,000	2,000
year 6	1/21 × $21,000	1,000
Total Depreciation		21,000

CHAPTER 11

Double Entry Records for Depreciation

Recording depreciation involves maintaining each non-current asset at its historical cost. Another ledger account where the depreciation to date is recorded is also kept. This account where depreciation to date is kept is called accumulated provision for depreciation account or accumulated depreciation account.

11.1 Double Entry Principles for depreciation:

Debit the statement of comprehensive income (profit and loss account)

Credit the accumulated provision for depreciation account

Example 1

A business has a financial year end of December 31. A computer was bought for $4,000 on January 1, 2008. It is to be depreciated at the rate of 20 percent per annum using the reducing balance method. Record the depreciation on double entry bookkeeping.

Solution:

Calculation of depreciation for the first three years using reducing balance method

		$
Cost as at Jan. 1, 2008		4,000
Depreciation, Dec.31, 2008	20% x 4,000	-800
Balance as Jan. 1, 2009		3,200
Depreciation, Dec.31, 2009	20% x 3,200	-640
Balance as Jan. 1,2010		2,560
Depreciation, Dec.31, 2010	20% x 2,560	-512

Balance as at Jan. , 2011   2,048

Computer Accounts

2008		$	
Jan. 1	Cash	4,000	

Accumulated Provision for depreciation Accounts

2008		$	2008		$
Dec. 31	Balance c/d	800	Dec.31	P&L	800
2009			2009		
Dec. 31	Balance c/d	1,440	Jan. 1	Balance b/d	800
			Dec.31	P&L	640
		1,440			1,440
2010			2010		
Dec.31	Balance c/d	1,952	Jan. 1	Balance b/d	1,440
			Dec.31	P&L	512
		1,952			1,952
			2011		
			Jan. 1	Balance b/d	1,952

NOTE:

P&L means profit and loss accounts

Statement of Comprehensive Income (Profit & Loss Accounts)

	$
2008	
Dec. 31 Acc. Prov. for depreciation	800
2009	
Dec. 31 Acc. Prov. for depreciation	640
2010	
Dec. 31 Acc. Prov. for depreciation	512

Statements of financial position (extracts)

As at Dec. 31, 2008	$	$
Computer at cost	4,000	
Accumulated Depreciation	-800	
		3,200

As at Dec. 31, 2009		
Computer at cost	4,000	
Accumulated Depreciation	-1,440	
		2,560

As Dec. 31, 2010		
Computer at cost	4,000	
Accumulated Depreciation	-1,952	
		2,048

11.2 The disposal of a Non-Current Asset

When a non-current asset is sold, we need to remove it from the ledger accounts. This can be done in the following ways:

a) The cost of the asset sold has to be removed from the asset accounts.
b) The accumulated depreciation of the asset sold has to be taken out of the accumulated provision for depreciation accounts.
c) The profit or loss on the asset sold has to be determined.

Accounting Entries needed

The following entries are needed for the sales of a non-current asset:

1. Transfer the cost of the asset sold to an asset disposal account:
Debit asset disposal account
Credit asset account

2. Transfer the accumulated depreciation already charged on the asset to asset disposal account:
Debit accumulated provision for depreciation account
Credit asset disposal account

3. For the amount received on disposal:
Debit bank or cash account
Credit asset disposal account

4. Transfer the difference (i.e. the amount required to balance the asset disposal account) to the statement of comprehensive income (profit and loss account)

a) If the asset disposal account shows a difference on the debit side(a credit balance):
Debit asset disposal account
Credit profit and loss account

b) If the asset disposal account shows a difference on the credit side (a debit balance):

Debit profit and loss account
Credit asset disposal account

ILLUSTRATION 1

Equipment costing $120,000 was bought on 1st January 2001. Depreciation was provided at 20% annually on a straight line method. It was sold on 30th June, 2004 for $31,500.

a) Calculate its accumulated depreciation at the time of sales

b) In the year of sales, profit or loss was

c) The net book value of the asset at the time of sale was

Solution:

a) $3.5 \times 20\% \times \$120,000 = \$84,000$

b)

Equipment Disposal Accounts

	$		$
		Accumulated	
Cost	120,000	Depreciation	84,000
		Cash	31,500
		P&L	4,500
	120,000		120,000

Profit was $4,500 in the year of sales.

		$
c) Cost		120,000
	Accumulated depreciation	(84,000)
	Net Book Value	36,000

ILLUSTRATION 2

The table below shows information concerning machinery imported from abroad.

	$
Purchase price of machinery	120,000
Import duty	11,000
Installation cost	5,500
Annual maintenance cost	1,400
Estimated useful life 5years	
Estimated scrap value	6,000

What is the total acquisition cost of the equipment?

What is the annual depreciation charged if straight line method is used?

Solution:

a.

	$
Purchase price of machinery	120,000
Import duty	11,000
Installation cost	5,500
	136,500

b. $\dfrac{136,500 - 6,000}{5}$ = $26,100

11.3 Changes of depreciation Method

It is possible to make a change in the calculation of depreciation. The change should not be frequent. Where a change to the depreciation is material, the effect of the change on the reported figure should be stated as a note to the financial statement in the year of the change.

CHAPTER 12

IMPAIRMENT OF ASSETS

12.1   Impairment of Assets

According to IAS 36, impairment of assets ensures that assets are not carried in the statement of financial position at more than their recoverable amount (i.e the higher of fair value less cost of disposal, and the value in use)

IAS 36 applies to the following assets:

1) Land
2) Buildings
3) Machinery and equipment
4) Investment property carried at cost
5) Intangible assets
6) Goodwill
7) Investments in subsidiaries, associates and joint ventures carried at cost
8) Assets carried at revalued, under IAS 16 and IAS 38

IAS 36 does not apply to the following assets

1) Inventories
2) Assets arising from construction contracts
3) Deferred tax assets
4) Assets arising from employees' benefits
5) Investment property carried at fair value
6) Agricultural assets carried at fair value
7) Financial assets
8) Insurance contract assets
9) Non-current assets held for sales

Key definitions are as follows:

12.1.1. Impairment Loss

Impairment loss is the amount by which the carrying amount of an asset in the statement of financial position is higher than the recoverable value of the asset.

12.1.2. Carrying amount

Carrying amount is the amount at which an asset is carried in the statement of financial position after deducting accumulated depreciation.

12.1.3. Recoverable amount

Recoverable amount is the higher of an asset fair value less cost of its disposal, and its value in use.

12.1.4. Fair Value

Fair value is the price that would be received to sell an asset or paid to transfer a liability in orderly transactions between market participants at the measurement date.

12.1.5. Value in Use

Value in use is the present value of the future cash flow expected to be derived from an asset or cash-generating unit.

12.1.6. Cash Generating Unit

Cash generating unit is a small group of identifiable assets from which cash inflow is expected.

12.2 How do we find out that there is impairment?

Every company shall watch out for external and internal indicators of a possible impairment.

12.2.1 External indicators: are significant decline in market value, significant adverse changes in technology, market, economic and legal environment, and where carrying amount of company's net assets exceeds market capitalization.

12.2.2. Internal indicators are: obsolescence or physical damage, internal evidence available that an asset's performance will be worse than expected, significant adverse changes to company including plans to discontinue or restructure an operation using the asset or to dispose of it earlier than planned.
Therefore, if the company finds any of these indicators, it should determine asset's recoverable amount and find out whether there is impairment.

The recoverable amounts of the following types of intangible assets are measured annually, whether or not there is an indication of impairment of assets:

- An intangible asset with an indefinite useful life

- An intangible asset not yet available for use

- Goodwill acquired in a business combination

Case Study 1

Jevta Ltd. has machinery that amounted to $70,000 after accumulated depreciation as at December 31, 2014. It is discovered that there was a decline in the market value of the machinery. The fair value of the asset as at December 31, 2014 was $65,000 and value in use of the asset was $55,000.

You are required to provide answers to the following questions:

1) What is the carrying amount

2) What is the recoverable value

3) Calculate impairment loss

4) Post the information above to journal

5) Record the asset in the statement of financial position

Solutions

1) The carrying amount of the machinery as at December 31, 2014, was $70,000.

2) The recoverable value is the higher of the fair value less cost to sale, and the value in use. The fair value ($65,000) is higher than the value in use ($55,000). Therefore, the recoverable value is $65,000.

3)

	$
Recoverable value	65,000
Carrying amount	-70,000
Impairment loss	5,000

4)

Journal Entry

	$	$
Income statement	5,000	
Machinery		5,000

Being the amount recorded for impairment loss

5)
Statement of financial position as at December 31, 2014

	$
Machinery	100,000
Less accumulated depreciation	(30,000)
	70,000
Less impairment loss	(5,000)
	65,000

12.3 How to Account for Impairment Loss

There are two models for accounting for impairment losses:

12.3.1. Cost Model

Debit: statement of comprehensive income

Credit : Asset account

12.3.2. Revaluation Model

Debit: Equity; revaluation surplus

Credit: asset account

Note:

If there is no positive balance figure on revaluation surplus, cost model should be used.

12.3.3. Reversal of Impairment Loss

Where there is an indication that impairment loss might have been decreased, reversal of impairment loss under cost model is always recognized.

Accounting entries for the reversal of impairment loss are as follows:

Debit: Asset accounts

Credit: statement of comprehensive income (P&L); Reversal of impairment loss

12.3.4. Recoverable Value of an Individual Asset and cash Generating Unit

If it is not possible to calculate the recoverable value of an individual asset, then the recoverable amount of the CGU (cash generating unit to which the asset belongs should be calculated. A CGU is a small group of identifiable assets that can generate cash inflow for an entity as a continuous use of the assets, and are independent of cash flow from other assets.

Any impairment loss calculated for a CGU should be allocated to reduce the carrying amount of the asset in the following order:

- the carrying amount of goodwill should be first reduced then the carrying amount of other assets of the unit should be reduced on a pro rata basis, which is determined by the relative carrying value of each asset; then
- any reductions in the carrying amount of the individual assets should be treated as impairment losses. The carrying amount of any individual asset should not be reduced below the highest of its fair value less cost to sell, its value in use, and zero.
- If this rule is applied then the impairment loss not allocated to the individual asset will be allocated on a pro rata basis to the other assets of the group.

Example
A cash-generating unit has the following net assets:

	$m
Goodwill	60
Property	120
Plant & Equipment	180
	360

A recoverable amount has been determined and is $270.

Allocate the impairment loss to the net asset of the entity.

Solution:

	Goodwill	Property	Plant	Total
	$m	$m	$m	$m
Carrying amount	60	120	180	360
Impairment loss	-60	-12	-18	-90
Carrying value after impairment	0	108	162	270

CHAPTER 13

13.0 REVALUATION OF FIXED ASSETS (NON-CURRENT ASSETS)

Revaluation of fixed assets is the process of increasing or decreasing their carrying amount in case of major changes in the market value of the fixed asset.

International Financial Reporting Standards stipulated that fixed assets should be initially recorded at cost, but they allow two models for subsequent accounting for fixed assets, namely cost model and revaluation model.

13.1. Cost Model

Under cost model, fixed assets are carried at historical cost less accumulated depreciation and accumulated impairment losses.

ILLUSTRATION 1

Samotex Ltd. purchased a building worth $100,000 on January 1, 2006. The building has a useful life of 10 years, and the company uses a straight line method of depreciation. What will be the value of the building at December 31, 2008 and accumulated depreciation for the period?

Record the above information in the book of accounts.

SOLUTION:

Step 1

The building will first be recorded at its historical cost.

Journal Entry

	$	$
Building	100,000	
Cash		100,000

Step 2

The historical cost of the building will be reduced by the accumulated deprecation and accumulated impairment loss of the building.

Calculation of accumulated depreciation:

$100,000/10 = $10,000$

Annual depreciation $= $10,000$

Accumulated depreciation as December 31, 2008:

$3 \times $10,000 = $30,000$

The carrying amount is $100,000 minus $30,000 which equals $70,000.

Statement of Financial Position as at December 31, 2008

	$
Non-current Assets (Fixed Assets)	
Buildings	100,000
Accumulated depreciation	(30,000)
Net Book value	70,000

We can see that the building remains at its historical cost, and is periodically depreciated with no other upward adjustment to value.

13.2   Revaluation Model

Under revaluation model, an asset is initially recorded at its historical cost, but subsequently adjusted for increase or decrease in value.

The only difference between the cost model and the revaluation model is that, the cost model only allows downward adjustment due to impairment losses while revaluation model allows both upward and downward adjustment in value of an asset.

ILLUSTRATION 2

Consider the illustration 1 of Samotex Ltd. as stated in case of cost model. Assume on December 31, 2008, the company intends to switch to revaluation model and carries out revaluation exercise which estimates the fair market value of the building to be $90,000 as at December 31, 2008. The carrying amount at the date is $70,000.

   a) What is the amount of upward adjustment if there is any?

   b) What is the revalued amount of the building?

SOLUTION:

a)

The upward amount:
= $ 90,000 - $70,000
= $20,000

b)
The revalued amount of the building is $90,000 because the carrying amount of $70,000 increased by $20,000.

Journal entry

$ $

Building	20,000	
Revaluation surplus		20,000

Being the value of the revaluation of asset

Note:

Upward revaluation is not considered as a normal gain and is not recorded in the income statement rather it is directly credited to equity account called revaluation surplus. Revaluation surplus contains all the upward revaluation of company's assets until all those assets are disposed off.

13.2.1 Depreciation after Revaluation

Depreciation in the periods after revaluation is based on the revalued amount. Under the illustration of Samotex Ltd., depreciation for 2009 shall be the new carrying amount divided by the remaining useful life ($90,000/7) which is equal to $12,857.14.

13.2.2. Reversal of Revaluation

If a revalued asset is subsequently valued down due to impairment, the loss is first written off against any available balance in the revaluation surplus and if the loss is higher than the balance in the revaluation surplus of the same asset, the difference is charged to the income statement as impairment loss.

ILLUSTRATION

Assume on December 31, 2010 Samotex Ltd. revalues the building again to find out that the fair value should be $60,000.

Carrying amount as at December 31, 2010 is $90,000 minus 2-year depreciation ($2\times12,857.14$) which amounts to $64,285.72.

The carrying amount exceeds the fair value by ($64,285.72 - $60,000) = $4,285.72 . The revaluation surplus should be reduced by $4,285.72. The company is already having $20,000 in the revaluation surplus account meant for the same asset. This $20,000 is sufficient to absorb the impairment loss ($4,285.72) and hence, there is no need to post the impairment loss to an income statement.

Journal Entry

	$	$
Revaluation Surplus	4,285.72	
Building Account		4,285.72

CHAPTER 14

14.0 CONTROL ACCOUNTS

14.1 Control

Control can be specifically classified into two main types in an organization. They are organizational control and control on the accounting data.

14.1.1 Organizational Control

It includes a segregation of duties and an authorization of payments. Examples of Organizational control are as follows:

1. The same person will not both invoice customers, and act as a cashier when payment is received.

2. If a member of staff claims reimbursement of expenses, the expenses should be authorized for payment by another member of staff.

3. Who has the authority to sell goods on credit in the organization should first be given approval to do so.

   All the aforementioned statements above are organizational controls because they do not impose control on accounting data. The first two statements are segregation of duties while the last statement is an authority or approval.

14.1.2 Control on Accounting Data

Control on accounting data is a control imposed on accounting data and information to ensure that they are free from errors, mistakes, and to ensure prevention and location of irregularities in accounting records. Some examples are bank reconciliation and control accounts.

Control accounts are used mainly in manual accounting system. Control accounts are needed to give management of an organization control over some aspects of a business. They facilitate a delegation of duties and provide a check on the work of the subordinates. They provide a means of locating and preventing errors.

When a business is still very small, all the accounts of the business can be kept in one ledger and a trial balance could be drawn up as a test of arithmetical accuracy of the accounting records. If the trial balance of a small business disagrees, its accounting books could be easily checked in order to locate the errors. The mere fact that the trial balance total is balance does not mean that the accounts are free from errors. Although, trial balance ensures that all double entry appear, at least to have been recorded correctly, there are still some errors that do not affect trial balance.

When a business entity is becoming larger, and the accounting work has been so divided up that there are several ledgers, location of any errors could be very difficult if trial balance was the only means used to locate and detect errors. Every item in every ledger may require to be verified just to find out one or more errors that caused the trial balance not to balance. What is needed is a type of trial balance for each ledger, and this requirement is met by control accounts.

Control accounts are often called total accounts, adjustments accounts or self balancing ledger system.

Purposes of Control Accounts

1. It is used to discover mistakes in the work of junior member of staff.
2. To facilitate easy detection of errors
3. To detect and prevent fraud
4. To know the account balance
5. To know credit sales or credit purchases

There are two types of control accounts. They are total accounts receivable accounts and total accounts payable accounts.

A control accounts for sales ledger can either be called total accounts receivable accounts or sales ledger control accounts. A control accounts for purchases ledger can either be called total accounts payable accounts or purchases ledger control accounts.

14.1.2.1 Sales Ledger Control Accounts

The format below could be used to prepare sales ledger control accounts:

Sales Ledger Control Accounts or Total Accounts Receivable Accounts

	$		$
Balance b/d	XX	Balance b/d	XX
Dishonored checks	XX	Discounts allowed	XX
Interest on overdue a/c	XX	Bad debts written off	XX
Refund to debtors	XX	Returns Inwards	XX
Sales journal	XX	Bank/Cash	XX
		Credit notes	XX
		Set off against purchases	XX
		Balance c/d	XX
	XX		XX
Balance b/d	XX		

Table 14.1.2.1 lists the sources of information used to draw up sales ledger control accounts.

Table 14.1.2.1

Sales Ledger Control Accounts	Sources of information
1. Opening accounts receivable	Total amount of debtors' balances at the end of the previous period
2. Credit sales	Total from the sales day book/sales journal
3. Return inwards	Total of the return inward day book

4. Check received	Cash book, bank column on debit side
5.Cash received	Cash book, cash column on debit side
6.Discounts allowed	Total of discounts allowed in the cash book
7.Closing accounts receivable	Total amount of debtors' balances at the end of the current period

ILLUSTRATION 14.1.2.1a

Sales ledger control account data of Biz Ltd for the month of January are as follows:

	$
Accounts receivable balance on January 1, 2012	3,788
Total credit sales for the month	20,580
Check received from customers for the month	14,568
Cash received from customers in the month	2,472
Returns inward from customers during the month	592
Accounts receivable balance on January 31, 2012 as extracted from sales ledger	6,736

SOLUTION

Total accounts receivable accounts

2012	$	2012	$
Jan. 1 Balance b/d	3,788	Jan. 31 Bank	14,568
Jan. 31 Sales	20,580	Jan. 31 Cash	2,472
		Jan. 31 Return inward	592
		Jan. 31 Balance c/d	6,736
	24,368		24,368
Balance b/d	6,736		

Note:

The sales ledger has been proved to be arithmetically correct because the control account balance is equal to the accounts receivable balance on January 31, 2012 as extracted from the sales ledger. In a nutshell, the sales ledger control accounts balance or total accounts receivable account is $6,736 and the sales ledger balance is $6,736.

In conclusion, the above control account proves that the sales ledger is free from error. This is one of the purposes of control accounts. Please refer to **14.1.2** for purposes of control accounts.

14.1.2.2 Purchases Ledger Control Accounts

The format below could be used to prepare purchases ledger control accounts.

Purchases Ledger Control Accounts or Total Accounts Payable Accounts

	$		$
Returned outwards	XX	Balance b/d	XX
Bank	XX	Purchase journal	XX
Cash	XX	interest on over due a/c	XX
Discounts received	XX		XX
Set off against sales	XX		
Debit Notes	XX		
Balance c/d	XX		
	XX		XX
		Balance b/d	XX

Table 14.1.2.2 lists the sources of information used to draw up purchase ledger control accounts.

Table 14.1.2.2

Purchases Ledger Control Accounts	Sources of information
1. Opening accounts Payable	List of the creditors' balances at the end of the previous period
2. Credit Purchases	Total from the purchases day book
3. Return outwards	Total of the return outwards day book
4. Check paid	Cash book, bank column on credit side
5.Cash paid	Cash book, cash column on credit side
6.Discounts received	Total of discounts received in the cash book
7.Closing accounts payable	List of all creditors' balances at the end of the current period

ILLUSTRATION 14.1.2.2a

Purchases Ledger Control accounts data:

	$
Accounts payable balance on Jan 1, 2012	4,000
Checks paid to suppliers during the month	3,730
Returns outwards to suppliers during the month	200
Bought from suppliers in the month	4,100
Accounts payable balance on January 31 as extracted from the purchase ledger	4,900

SOLUTION

Total Accounts Payable Accounts

2012	$	2012	$
		Jan. 1 accounts	
Jan 31 Bank	3,730	payable	4,000
Jan. 31 Returns			
outwards	200	Jan 31 purchases	4,750
Jan. 31 Balance c/d	4,900		
	8,830		8,750

Total accounts payable accounts show that there is $80 difference between debit and credit sides. We can say there is an error in purchases ledger provided all the data in the original books of accounts are correctly transferred to the purchases ledger.

We need to check in details the purchases ledger to discover the error.

14.1.2.3 Reasons for Two Accounting Balances

There may be debit balance on the sales ledger as well as credit balance. For example, if we sold goods worth $800 to M. Morgan, he then paid in full for the goods, and then returned $80 worth of goods to us. This would leave a credit balance of $80 on the account, whereas usually the balance in the sales ledger is debit balance.

ILLUSRATTION 14.1.2.3

	$
2013	
Dec. 1 Sales ledger - debit balances	7,632
Dec. 1 Sales ledger - credit balances	44
Dec. 31 Transaction for the month:	
cash received	208
checks received	

	12,478
Sales	14,180
bad debts written off	612
allowance for doubtful debt	350
discount allowed	596
returns inwards	1,328
cash refunded to a customer for overpayment	74
Dishonored check	58
interest charged by us on over due debt	100
at the end of the month:	
sales ledger - debit balance	6,858
Sales ledger - credit balance	80

SOLUTION

Total Accounts Receivable Accounts

2013	$	2013	$
Dec.1 Balance b/f	7632	Dec. 1 Balance b/f	44
Dec. 31 sales	14,180	Dec. 31 cash	208
Dec. 31 cash refunded	74	Dec. 31 Bank	12478
Dec. 31 Dishonored check	58	Dec. 31 Bad debt written off	612
Dec. 31 interest on debt	100	Dec. 31 Discount allowed	596
Balance c/d	80	Dec. 31 Return inwards	1,328

		Balance c/d	6,858
	22,124		22,124

Note that you do not set-off the debit and credit balance in the sales ledger.

14.1.4 Contra Accounts

A contra account is a situation whereby the same entity is both a supplier and a customer, and inter-indebtedness is set off. This contra entry is needed to be entered in the control accounts.

Here is an example

i.   A business has sold goods worth $700 to A. Eunice
ii.   A. Eunice has supplied the business with goods worth $1,000.
iii.   The $700 owing by A. Eunice is set off against $1,000 owed to her.
iv.   This leaves $300 owing to her in the business accounts.

Solution
In the book of the business

Sales Ledger

A. Eunice Accounts

	$		$
Sales	700		

Purchases Ledger

	A. Eunice	
$		$
	Purchases	1,000

Set-off now takes place following the preparation of journal entries.

Sales Ledger
A. Eunice

	$		$
Sales	700	Set-off purchases ledger	700

Purchases Ledger
A. Eunice

	$		$
Set-off sales ledger	700	Purchases	1,000
Balance c/d	300		
	1000		1,000

ILLUSTRATION 14.1.4

The trial balance of Big Boss Ltd revealed a difference in the books. In order that the errors could be located it was decided to prepare purchases and sales ledger control accounts.

From the following information, prepare the control accounts and show where an error might have been made:

2011	$
Jan. 1 Purchases ledger balances	19,420
Jan. 1 Sales ledger balances	28,227
Total for the year 2011	
Purchases journal	210,416
Sales journal	305,824
Returns outwards journal	1,452
Returns inwards journal	3,618
Checks paid to suppliers	205,419
Petty cash paid to suppliers	62
Checks received from customers	287,317
Discounts allowed	4,102
Discounts received	1,721
Balances on the sales ledger set off against balance in the purchases	640

Dec. 31 the list of balances in the purchases ledger shows a total of $20,210 and the list of balances in the sales ledger shows a total of $38,374.

SOLUTION

Sales Ledger Control Accounts

2011	&	2011	$
Jan. 1 Balance b/f	28,227	Return inward journal	3,618
Jan. 31 Sales journal	305,824	Bank & cash	287,317
		Discount allowed	4,102
		Set-off against purchases	
		Ledger	640
		Balance c/d	38,374
	334,051		334,051
Balance b/d	38,374		

Purchases Ledger Control Accounts

2011	&	2011	$
Jan. 31 return outward	1,452	Jan. 1 Balance b/d	19,420
Jan. 31 Bank	205,419	Jan. 31 purchases journal	210,416
Jan. 31 Cash	62		
Jan. 31 Discount received	1,721		
Jan. 31 set-off balance	640		
Balance c/d	20,542		
	229,836		229,836
Balance b/d	20,542		

NOTE:

The balance of the purchases ledger control accounts at the end of the month is $20,542. This is different from the balance of the purchases ledger $20,210. It means that there is an error of $332 in the purchases ledger.

CHAPTER 15

15.0 BANK RECONCILIATION STATEMENT

Any organization that has a bank account must have bank column in its cash book. Every transaction of the organization with its bank must be recorded in its cash book (bank column). The bank also must record every transaction that transpires between its customers or account holders and the bank itself.

At the end of an accounting period, the bank balance in the customer's cash book has to be equal to the bank balance in the bank statement/records. If the two records are equal at each accounting period, there would be no need for the preparation of bank reconciliation statement.

Where there is a discrepancy between the bank balance in the cash book as prepared by the account holder and the bank balance in the bank statement as prepared by the bank, there will be a need to reconcile the two records.

15.1 What is Bank Reconciliation Statement?

Bank reconciliation statement is a statement that is prepared in order to make bank balance as shown in the cash book to be equal to bank balance as shown in the bank statement.

15.1.1 Items that May Cause Disagreements

The following are the items that can cause disagreements between bank balance as shown by the cash book and the bank balance as shown by the bank statement:

a) Bank charges, interest on loan, COT
b) Standing order
c) Credit transfer
d) Dishonored check

a) Bank Charges: These are deductions made by banks for services rendered to the customers/account holders.
b) Standing order: This is referred to as the payment effected by the bank on the customers standing instruction.
c) Credit transfer: This is the amount paid directly into the bank account of the account holder by its customers
d) Dishonored Check: These are the check paid into the bank upon receipt from customers but subsequently dishonored for one reason or the other.

Note:

The items (a) to (d) frequently appear in the bank statement but not in the cash book.

15.1.2   Other items that Cause Disagreements.

Other items that cause discrepancies between bank balance reflected in the cash book and the bank balance in the bank statement are as follows:

(i)   Outstanding check or unpresented Check: These are the checks issued by the bank account holder but yet to be presented by the payee.

(ii) Uncredited Check: These are the checks deposited by the accounts holder but yet to be credited by the bank as at the time the bank statement is being reconciled with the cash book (bank column only). These checks were paid to the accounts holder by its customers, but the bank is yet to credit the accounts holder's accounts when they were deposited by the accounts holder.

15.1.3 Errors in the Accounts

Errors in the cash book or bank statement can also cause disagreement between the cash book and bank statement. Sometimes, payment may be erroneously posted as receipts or a payment of $45 may be mistakenly recorded as $54 in either the cash book or bank statement.

15.2 Preparation of Bank Reconciliation Statement

The first thing to do before the preparation of bank reconciliation statement is to make an adjustment to cash book in order to accommodate the missing transactions and correction of errors so that an up-to-date balance could be derived.

15.2.1 Adjusted Cash Book

Adjusted cash book can be prepared using two different methods

First Method

Steps to be followed in preparing adjusted cash book are as follows:

1. Record all the items in the cash book to the adjusted cash book except the balance c/d.

2. All items in the bank statement that are not in the cash book (bank column only) should be recorded in the adjusted cash book. Items such as bank charges, credit transfer, standing order and dishonored check can be found in the bank statement but cannot be found in the cash book. All these items should be recorded in the adjusted cash book in order to up-date it. If there are any cash book errors or bank statement errors, they should be adjusted in the adjusted cash book.

Second Method

Steps to be followed in preparing adjusted cash book are as follows:

1. Start the adjusted cash book by recording the balance carried down (closing balance) in the cash book as a balance f/d (opening balance) in the adjusted cash book.

2. All items in the bank statement that are not in the cash book (bank column only) should be recorded in the adjusted cash book. Items such as bank charges, credit transfer, standing order and dishonored check can be found in the bank statement but cannot be found in the cash book. All these items should be recorded in the adjusted cash book. If there are any cash book errors or bank statement errors, they should be adjusted in the adjusted cash book.

NOTE:

If the debit side of the adjusted cash book is greater than its credit side, there is a debit balance and is positive.

If the credit side of the adjusted cash book is greater than its debit side, there is a credit balance and is negative, normally called bank overdraft.

The only difference between the two methods can be found in the "step 1"

15.2.2 Bank Reconciliation Statement

Bank reconciliation statement is prepared after adjusted cash book has been prepared.

A typical format of a bank reconciliation statement is as follows:

	$
Balance as per adjusted cash book(Debit balance)	XX
Add: Unpresented check/outstanding check	XX
	XX
Less: Uncredited check	(XX)
Balance as per bank statement	XX

ILLUSTRATION 15.2a

Cash Book (Bank column only) before adjustments on 31/12/2014

2014		$	2014		$
Dec. 1	Balance b/d	500	Dec. 5	J. James	130
Dec. 20	P. Thomas	200	Dec. 27	A. Eunice	350
Dec. 28	P. Jane	380	Dec. 31	Balance c/d	600
		1,080			1,080
Jan.1, 2015 Balance b/d		600			

Bank Statement for the period 31/12/2014

2014	Withdrawals $	Deposit $	Balance $
Dec.1 Balance b/d			500
Dec. 8 J. James(11825)	130		370
Dec. 21 Deposit		200	570
Dec. 28 Deposit		380	950

Dec. 29 A. Eunice(11826)	350		600
Dec. 30 Credit transfer		140	740
Dec. 31 Bank charges	100		640

You are required to prepare adjusted cash book for the period ended 31st December 2014.

SOLUTION

Identify those items that are in the bank statement but that are not in the cash book, record those items in the cash book (bank column). This new cash book will be called adjusted cash book as earlier explained. The items are as follows:

1. Credit transfer of $140, should be recorded on the debit side of the adjusted cash book.
2. Bank charges of $100. This amount should be credited to the adjusted cash book.

Adjusted cash book as at 31 December, 2014

2014		$	2014	$
Dec. 1	Balance b/d	500	Dec. 5 J. James	130
Dec. 20	P. Thomas	200	Dec. 27 A. Eunice	350
Dec. 24	P. Jane	380	Dec. 31 Bank charges*	100
Dec. 30	credit transfer*	140	Balance c/d	640
		1,220		1,220
	Balance b/d	640		

The balance as per adjusted cash book is $640. This is equal to balance as per bank statement of $640. Prepare bank reconciliation to prove the equality in the two balancing figures ($640).

Identify those items in the cash book, but that are not in the bank statement. These items will be used to prepare bank reconciliation statement. It could be seen in the records that there are no items in the cash book that are not in the bank statement, and hence the adjusted cash book balance is equal to the bank statement balance.

Bank reconciliation statement as at 31 December, 2014

	$
Balance as per adjusted cash book	640
Add: Unpresented checks	0
Less: Uncredited checks	0
Balance as per bank statement	640

15.3 Bank Balance

The balance to be recorded in the statement of financial position as bank balance is the balance as per adjusted cash book.

15.4 Bank Overdrafts

A bank overdraft is a credit balance in the cash book (bank column only). It is a negative balance. The same procedures used earlier, should be used in reconciling cash book balance (bank overdraft) with the bank balance in the bank statement. The only difference is that the bank overdraft balance will be shown as a negative figure.

A format of Bank reconciliation statement when there is a bank overdraft balance is stated below:

Bank reconciliation statement as at the month ending

	$
Balance as per adjusted cash book(bank overdraft)	(XX)
Add: Unpresented checks	XX
Less: Uncredited checks	(XX)
Balance as per bank statement	XX

ILLUSTRATION 15.4a

The bank statement for R. Thomas for the month of May 2015 is:

2015	Dr.	Cr.	Balance
	$	$	$
May 1 Balance b/d			(8,400)
May 8 J. Morgan	368		(8,768)
May 16 Check		584	(8,184)
May 20 W. Williams	320		(8,504)
May 21 Check		738	(7,766)
May 31 G. Frank:credit transfer		176	(7,590)
May 31 Standing order	64		(7,654)
May 31 Bank charges	38		(7,692)

The cash book for the Month of May 2015

2015 $		2015 $

May 16 A Eunice	584	May 1 Balance b/d	8,400
May 21 J. James	738	May 6 J. Morgan	368
May 31 J. Jasper	384	May 30 W. Williams	320
May 31 Balance c/d	8,390	May 30 K. Paul	1,008
	10,096		10,096
		June1,2015 Balance b/d	8,390

SOLUTION

Adjusted cash book for the period 31st May, 2015

2015	$	2015	$
May 16 A Eunice	584	May 1 Balance b/d	8,400
May 21 J. James	738	May 6 J. Morgan	368
May 31 J. Jasper	384	May 30 W. Williams	320
May 31 G. Frank: credit transfer	176	May 30 K. Paul	1,008
May 31 Balance c/d	8,316	May 31 Standing order	64
		May 31 Bank charges	38
	10,198		10,198
		June 1,2015 Balance b/d	8,316

Bank Reconciliation Statement as at 31st May, 2015

	$
Balance as per adjusted cash book	(8,316)
Add: Unpresented checks	1008
	(7,308)
Less: Uncredited checks	-384
Balance as per bank statement	(7,692)

15.5 Benefits of Bank Reconciliation Statement

Benefits and purposes of bank reconciliation are as follows:

1. To ensure that all cash recorded as deposits in the cash book is actually lodged in the bank.

2. To know the actual amount of payment made directly by customers into the bank accounts

3. To discover whether the account holder has been overcharged in terms of bank charges

Illustration

The following trial balance was extracted from the book of Mr. James at the close of business on February 28, 2010.

	Dr $	Cr $
Purchases and sales	92,800	157,165
Cash at bank	4,100	
Cash in hand	324	
Capital Account 1 March 2009		11,400
Drawings	17,100	
Office Furniture	2,900	
Rent	3,400	
Wages & Salaries	31,400	

Discounts	820	160
Accounts receivable and accounts payable	12,316	5,245
Inventory March 1, 2009	4,120	
Allowance for doubtful debts 1 March 2009		405
Delivery van	3,750	
Van running costs	615	
Bad debts written off	730	
	174,375	174,375

Additional information 1
   a. Inventory as at February 28, 2010, $2,400.
   b. Wages and salaries accrued at February 28, 2010 $340.
   c. Rent prepaid at February 28, 2010 $230.
   d. Van running costs owing at February 28, 2010 $72.
   e. Increase the allowance for doubtful debts by $91.
   f. Provide for depreciation as follows: Office furniture $380.
       Delivery van $1,250.

Additional information 2

It was discovered that as at February 28, 2010 that cash at bank as reflected by cash book was $4,100 but cash at bank shown by bank statement was $4,880.

The following were found in the bank statement but not in the cash book:
   1. February 26, 2010; bank Charges $120
   2. February 27, 2010; direct credit transfer by Mr. John, a customer $2,000
   3. February 28, 2010; standing order based on the instruction of Mr. James to pay a supply $1,000

The following were found in the cash book but not in the bank statement:
1. Outstanding check (unpresented check) $500
2. Uncredited check $600

You are required to prepare the following:
1. Income statement for the year ended February 28, 2010
2. Statement of financial position as at February 28, 2010
3. Bank reconciliation statement as at February 28, 2010

Suggested solution

Mr. James

(1) Income Statement for the year ended February 28, 2010

	Note	$	$	$
Sales				157,165
Less Cost of Sales				
Opening Stock			4,120	
Purchases			92,800	
			96,920	
Less Closing stocks			(2,400)	
Cost of sales			94,520	(94,520)
Gross profit				62,645
Discount received				160
				62,805
Less Expenses				
Wages & Salaries	1		31,740	
Rent	2		3,170	

Van running costs	3	687	
Allowance for doubtful debts	4	91	
Discounts allowed		820	
Bank charges (C.O.T)		120	
Bad debts written off		730	
Depreciation:			
Office Furniture	380		
Delivery van	1,250		
	1,630	1,630	
		38,988	(38,988)
Net profit			23,817

(2) Statement of Financial Position as at February 28, 2010

	Note	$	$	$
Non-Current Assets				
Office furniture			2,900	
Less: Depreciation			(330)	
			2,520	2,520
Delivery van			3,750	
Less: Depreciation			(1 250)	
			2,500	2,500
Current Assets				
Inventory			2,400	
Accounts receivable	5		9,320	

Rent prepaid		230	
Cash at bank	6	4,980	
Cash in hand		<u>324</u>	
A		17,754	

Current liabilities

Accounts payable	7		4,245	
Accrued Expenses:				
Wages and salaries		340		
Van running expenses		<u>72</u>		
		412	<u>412</u>	
B			(4,657)	
Working capital (A - B)				<u>13,097</u>
				<u>18,117</u>

Capital		11,400	
Net profit		<u>23,817</u>	
		35,217	
Less: Drawings		<u>(17,100)</u>	_____
		18,117	<u>18,117</u>

(3)Bank Reconciliation Statement as at February 28, 2010

	$
Balance as per adjusted cash book (Note 6)	4,980
Add: Outstanding check	

	500
	5,480
Less: Uncredited check	(600)
Balance as Per Bank Statement	4,880

Workings:

Note 1

Wages and salaries

Date 2010		$	Date 2010		$
Feb. 28	Bank	31,400	Feb. 28	Income stat.	31,740
Feb. 28	Balance c/d	340			
		31,740			31,740
				Balance b/b	340

Note 2

Rent Account

Date 2010		$	Date 2010		$
Feb. 28	Bank	3,400	Feb. 28	Income stat.	3,170
			Feb. 28	Balance c/d	230
		3,400			3,400
	Balance b/d	230			

Note 3

Van running costs

Date 2010		$	Date 2010		$
Feb. 28	Bank	615	Feb. 28	Income stat.	687
Feb. 28	Balance c/d	72			
		687			687
			Balance b/d		72

Note 4

Allowance for doubtful debts

Date 2010		$	Date 2010 March, 1 2009		$
				Balance b /f	405
Feb. 28	Balance c/d	496	Feb. 28	Income stat.	91
		496			496
			Balance b/d		496

Note 5

Accounts Receivable Accounts

Date 2010		$	Date 2010		$
Feb. 28	Balance	12,316	Feb. 27	Bank	2,000
				Allowance for doubtful debt	496
				Balance c/d	9,820
		12,316			12,316
	Balance b/d	9,820			

Note 6
Adjusted Cash Book as at February 28, 2010

Date	Particulars	Folio	Bank	Date	Particulars	Folio	Bank
2010			$	2010 Feb.			$
				26	Bark charges		120
Feb.					Standing		
28	Balance b/f		4,100		crder		1,000
Feb.	Direct						
27	transfer		2,000		Balance c/d		4,980
			6,100				6,100
	Balance b/d		4,980				

Review Questions 1

Accounting equation/Double Entry Bookkeeping

1. The basic accounting equation is
   A. Assets + Liabilities
   B. Assets = Equity – Liability
   C. Equity + Assets = Liabilities
   D. Liabilities = Assets – Equity

2. C. Palic is setting up a business. $5,000 is deposited in a bank account. Out of this amount, $650 is borrowed from friends while the remaining balance is his personal money. Calculate the total asset.

   A. $4,450
   B. $650
   C. $5,000
   D. $4,350

3. Mr. Stone started business with $1,900 on February 1, 2012. He made a net loss of $60 at the end of the year. How much is his capital at the beginning of the year 2013?
   A. $1,900
   B. $1,840
   C. $1,960
   D. $2,060

4. Miss Eunice started a business with $2,500 on January 2010. She earned a net profit of $1,019 at the end of 2010. How much will her capital be at January 1, 2011?
   A. $1,019
   B. $1,901
   C. $2,500
   D. $3,519

5. Payment of expenses---------- assets

   A. devalues

B. increases
C. reduces
D. change

6. Payment of account payable --------

    A. increases assets and reduces liabilities
    B. increase assets and increases liabilities
    C. decreases assets and decreases liabil:ties
    D. decrease liability and equate asset

7. What effect will an increase in capital have on assets?

    A. increase assets
    B. decrease assets
    C. no effect
    D. equate asset

8. The basic accounting equation is -----

    A. capital + asset = liability
    B. capital = liability + asset
    C. capital = liability + asset
    D. asset = capital + liability

9. Capital decreases if -------- decreases

    A. Revenue
    B. Expense
    C. Liability
    D. Drawings

10. Accounting equation can be best related to-------

    A. income
    B. assets
    C. principles of double entry book-keeping
    D. nominal accounts

11. A business has the following items in it.

Building?
Cash $15,000
Plant & Machinery $300,000
 Debtors $60,000
Owner's equity $500,000
Loan $250,000
Creditors $25,000

What is the value of the building?

    A. $500,000
    B. $775,0000
    C. $400,000
    D. $450,000

12. Which of the following is not a current asset?

    A. Inventory
    B. Short- term investment
    C. Cash at bank
    D. Bank overdraft

13. Which of the following is not an asset?

    A. Cash
    B. Cash at bank
    C. Account receivable
    D. Tax owed

14. A business has the following items in it.
    Mortgage loan $40,000
    Account payable $15,000
    Account receivable $20,000
    Machinery $200,000
    Land and Building $520,000
    Owner's equity?

What is the value of owner's equity?

A. $658,000
B. $688,000
C. $685,000
D. $720,000

15. A business entity has the following in it

Capital $65,000
Asset ?
Liability $15,000

What is the value of Asset?

A. $70,000
B. $65,000
C. $90,000
D. $80,000

16. An investment of additional cash into a business enterprise results in a/an

A. Increase in asset and increase in capital
B. Decrease in capital and increase in cash
C. Decrease in capital and increase in loan
D. Increase in capital and decrease in cash

17. One of the following stands as a separate item in the basic accounting equation.

A. Owners equity
B. Asset
C. Account receivable
D. Liability

18. Owner's equity has what type of balance?

A. Debit balance
B. Credit balance
C. Negative balance
D. Positive balance

19. Which of the following is an expanded accounting equation for a sole proprietorship?
   A. Assets = Capital + Liabilities
   B. Assets = Owner's capital+ Liabilities
   C. Assets = Liabilities + Owner's equity+ Revenue – Expenses – Owner's drawings
   D. Capital = Asset + Liability – Drawings

20. A change in any item of a basic accounting equation will have effect on how many items
   A. Only three
   B. At least one
   C. Non of the items
   D. Four

21. Outstanding rent of $600 is paid by the proprietor. The effect on the balance sheet is ------
   A. Both asset and liability remain unchanged
   B. Liability is increased while the asset remain unchanged
   C. Capital Increased while liability decreased
   D. Liability increased while the asset decreased

22. Which of the following will be posted to the proprietor's capital accounts?
   A. Anticipated profit   B. Gross profit   C. Net profit
   D. Net sales

23. Steven's capital at January 1, 1999 and December 31, 1999 were $80,000 and $110,000 respectively. During the year he introduced additional capital of $13,500 and withdrew $8,500 for private use. What is his profit for the year ended January 31, 1999?
   A. $25,000 B.$30,000 C.$96,500 D. $93,500

24. The financial position of an enterprise at a particular time can be ascertained from
  A. Statement of cash flow
  B. Balance sheet
  C. Profit and loss accounts
  D. income statement

25. When a transaction causes an asset account to increase, there is an increase of equal amount in capital or
  A. a decrease of equal amount in the owner's equity account
  B. an increase of equal amount in a liability account
  C. an increase of equal amount in another asset account
  D. a decrease of equal amount in a liability account.

26. To realize an asset means to
  A. use it as collateral
  B. to turn it to cash
  C. to remove it from the company
  D. to evaluate it

27. Which of the following cannot be realized?
  A. machinery   B. debtors   C. Goodwill   D. creditors

28. The golden rule of double entry principles states that----------
  A. Debit and credit entry must be recorded and vice versa
  B. For each debit entry there must be a corresponding credit entry and vice versa.
  C. Debit entry must be recorded before credit entry
  D. Assets = Liabilities + Owner's equity

29. Double entry system is ------------
  A. A reporting system
  B. An accounting system
  C. A recording system
  D. Credit and debit entry system

30. How do you record cash invested in business by an entrepreneur, in a book of accounts
   B. Debit investment account and credit cash account
   C. Debit cash account and credit investment account
   D. Debit cash account and credit capital account
   E. Debit owner's equity and debit investment account

Review Questions 2

From the following trial balance of Jane Enterprise, prepare income statement for the year ending December 31, 2013, and statement of financial position as at that date, taking into consideration the adjustments shown below:

Trial Balance as at December 31, 2013

	Dr.	Cr.
	$	$
Sales		200,000
Purchases	175,000	
Sales returns	2,500	
Purchases returns		3,100
Opening Inventory at January 1, 2013	50,000	
Allowance for doubtful debts		400
Wages & Salaries	15,000	
Rates	3,000	
Telephone	500	
Shop Fittings at cost	20,000	
Van at cost	15,000	
Accounts receivable & Accounts payable		

	4,900	3,500
Bad Debts	100	
Capital		89,500
Bank Balance	1,500	
Drawings	9,000	
	296,500	296,500

i.   Closing inventory at December 31, 2013 $60,000.
ii.   Accrued wages $2,500.
iii. Rates prepaid $250
iv.   The allowance for doubtful debts to be increased to 10 per cent of accounts receivable.
v.   Telephone accounts outstanding $110
vi.   Depreciate shop fittings at 10 per cent per annum, and van at 20 per cent per annum, on cost.

Solution to Review Questions 1

1) The correct answer is:

D. Liabilities = Assets − Equity

2) The correct answer is B. $1,840.
The capital at the beginning of year 2013 will be:
Capital at February 1, 2012 − Net loss
= $1,900 − $60
= $1,840
Note: Net loss is always deducted from the opening capital to get the closing capital because net loss has a negative value.

3) The correct answer is D) $3,519
Capital at January 1, 2011 = capital at January 1, 2010 + Net loss
= $2,500 + $1,019
= $ 3,519

Note: Net profit is always added to opening capital because it is a positive figure.

4) The correct answer is C) reduces
Payment of expenses will definitely reduce assets. You can either pay by cash or bank. Bank and cash are assets from which expenses could be paid from. Either of these two will be reduced whenever there is a payment.

5) The right answer is C) decreases assets and decreases liabilities.
Payment of account payable will reduce asset. It will also reduce liability because account payable is a liability and once is paid for, it reduces.

Look at the accounting equation here:

Asset = Capital + Liability

The asset reduces by the amount paid out of asset (cash or bank) and liability also reduces by the amount of the liability (account payable) that was paid. This will be more explained under "double entry principles of accounts"

6) The correct answer is A) increase assets
The solution can also be picked from the above equation. If capital increases, assets must also increase. This will be more explained in double entry principles of accounts.

7) The correct answer is D) asset = capital + liability

8) The correct answer is A) Revenue

9) The correct answer is C) principles of double entry book-keeping

11) This question can be solved by a basic accounting equation

ASSETS	$
Building	?
Cash	15,000
Plant and Machinery	300,000
Debtors	60,000
	375,000

LIABILITIES	$
Loan	250,000

Creditors   25,000
                    275,000

ASSETS = CAPITAL + LIABILITY
Building + $375,000 = $500,000 + $275,000
Building + $375,000 = $775,000
  Building   = $775,000 - $375,000
                   = $400,000

The correct answer is C) $400,000

12) The correct answer is D) Bank overdraft

13) The correct answer is D) Tax owed
14) The correct answer is C) $685,000
The accounting equation can be used to solve this question.
Assets = Capital +Liabilities

Owner's Equity = Assets – Liabilities

Assets	$
Account receivable	20,000
Machinery	200,000
Land and building	520,000
	740,000

Liabilities	$
Mortgage loan	40,000
Accounts payable	15,000
	55,000

Owner's Equity = $740,000 – $55,000
                = $685,000
15) The answer is D) $80,000
The basic accounting equation can be used to solve this equation

Assets = Capital + Liabilities
Assets = $65,000 +$15,000
= $ 80,000

16) A) Increase in asset and increase in capital
17) B) Asset
18) B) credit balance
19) The answer is C)
    Assets = Liabilities + Owner's equity+ Revenue – Expenses –
Owner's drawings

20) B	26. B
21) C	27. D
22) C	28. B
23) A	29. C
24) B	30. C

Solution to Review Questions 2

Jane Enterprise

Income Statement for the year ended December 31, 2013

	$	$	$
Sales			200,000
Less Returns			(2,500)
			197,500
Less cost of Sales			
Opening stock		50,0C0	
Purchases	175,000		
Less purchases returns	(3,100)		
		171,900	
Cost of goods available		221,900	
Less Closing Inventory			

		(60,000)
Cost of Sales	161,900	(161,900)
Gross profit		35,600
Less Expenses:		
Allowance for doubtful debts	90	
Wages & Salaries	17,500	
Rates	2,750	
Telephone	610	
Bad Debts	100	
Depreciation:		

Shop Fittings	2,000		
Van	3,000		
		5,000	(26,050)
Net Profit			9,550

Statement of Financial Position as at December 31, 2013

	$	$	$
Non-current assets			
Shop Fittings	20,000		
Less Depreciation	(2,000)		
		18,000	
Van	15,000		
Less Depreciation	3,000		
		12,000	

		30,000	
Current Assets			
Inventory		60,000	
Accounts receivable	4,900		
Less Allowance for doubtful debt	(490)		
		4,410	
Prepaid rates		250	
Bank		1 500	
		65,160	
Current Liabilities			
Accounts payable	3,500		
Accrued wages	2,500		
Expenses Accrued	110		
		(6,110)	
Working capital		60,050	60,050
Net Assets			90,050
Capital		89,500	
Net profit		9,550	
		99,050	
Less Drawings		(9,000)	
		90,050	90,050

Workings

Wages and Salaries

2013		$	2013		
Dec. 31	Bank	15,000	Dec.31	Income Stat.	17,500
Dec. 31	Accrual c/d	2,500			
		17,500			17,500
			Bal. b/d		2,500

Rates Accounts

2013		$	2013		$
Dec. 31	Bank	3,000	Dec.31	Income Stat.	2,750
				Prepayment c/d	250
		3,000			3,000
	Balance b/d	250			

Allowance for doubtful debts

2013		$	2013		$
				Balance b/f	400
Dec. 31	Balance c/d	490	Dec. 31	Income Stat.	90
		490			490
				Balance b/d	490

Telephone Accounts

2013		$	2013		$
Dec. 31	Bank	500			
Dec. 31	Balance c/d	110	Dec. 31	Income Stat.	610
		610			610
				Balance b/d	110

REFERENCES:

Frank Wood (12th edition) Business Accounting

Toye Adelaje (2015) Basic Financial Accounting

Toye Adelaja (2015) Adjustment for Financial Statements

www.accountinghour.com

www.ingramcontent.com/pod-product-compliance
Lightning Source LLC
Chambersburg PA
CBHW070317190526
45169CB00005B/1657